Dave —
It's <u>NOT</u> in the
mechanics !
Play well

Jon Taylor

Golf Can't be this Simple

The Swing

Students Praise Concept Golf

"Concept Golf is about taking a few basic fundamentals and then allowing the golfer to become a better player. To play golf you must be able to score, not change your swing after every bad shot. Concept Golf allowed me to regain my confidence and to focus on the game of golf, not my swing.

In closing, I would highly recommend Concept Golf to anyone who wants to improve his golf game."

Kent Shumate, PGA Golf Professional
Mount Airy Country Club
Mount Airy, NC

"The way you teach is simple; but it's so simple that it's almost genius. My handicap went down a full five strokes within just the first couple of weeks after our lessons. I've added significant distance to my shots.

I can't recommend your approach highly enough. You're on to something great. Keep it up."

Bruce Deerson, Attorney
Raleigh, NC

"Fate intervened with my invitation to attend your golf camp on July 13, 14 and 15. In my association with this game, I have never had a more enjoyable and rewarding time. The fun and satisfaction I am now enjoying far surpasses what I ever thought was attainable for me. Your introduction to the "sensible" fundamentals contrasted all the previous fundamentals I was taught. Those never really made sense or felt right. With your instruction skills and encouragement it was as though I was led out of darkness. Played with the application of your fundamentals, this truly is a simple game that anyone can enjoy."

Den Brown, President
Delta Dental of Wisconsin
Stevens Point, WI

"Since you were here, I've posted three rounds at my club and played a pretty prestigious match-play tournament at Colonial Country Club in Harrisburg. The rounds I posted were 70, 71, 68. I won the match-play event by qualifying with a 68 and then winning all four of my matches. I played a total of 85 holes in that tournament and only made four bogeys.

You taught me how to "GOLF MY BALL!" I didn't want someone to tell me how to swing the club. I wanted someone to show me how to PLAY golf and that is exactly what you did."

Rick Troutman, President
RT Cleaners
Annville, PA

"Your instructions were as radical as I could have imagined. Concepts like relaxation, thinking to the target, placing all my weight on my right foot, and not keeping my left arm straight were as revolutionary as 'there is no Santa Claus.' If this was not enough you said 'golf is easy.' How could anything that is so analyzed, dissected and practiced be easy?

At 54, I am hitting the ball farther and straighter than ever. I swing with confidence and ease and am enjoying the game of golf for the first time."

Skip Lawrence, Artist
Mt. Airy, MD

"This has renewed my enthusiasm for the game. I now understand what the swing and the game is all about.

It was a great three days."

John Prais, Vice President Sales
Worzalla Publishing
Stevens Point, WI

"So...two firsts, two seconds and a third place, also a 'most improved' this year -- I think I owe you a prize!"

Carol Blair
Lexington, VA

"I have used several instructors, and you have been the best by far. Your explanations of the golf swing make your instructions easy to execute."

Michael Della-Rosa
Raleigh, NC

"The game is getting more and more fun since I took your course. I wish I could pass my knowledge on to my playing partners who struggle with: 'don't look up,' 'pushing the ball with your arms,' 'keeping weight on the left foot' and all sorts of mechanical details - details I have happily found I can now live without."

Marty Broadhurst
Sheperdstown, WV

"I had the competitive round of my life. Shot 75 on the Carolina in Southern Pines. Shot 40/35. This is a breakthrough round for me. My mind was completely focused on target, not on mechanics, and my swing from tee into the hole was smooth and relaxed."

Ray Kenny
Cary, NC

"Thanks for all your help. I never enjoyed golf until I had lessons from you."

Alex Powers, Artist
Myrtle Beach, SC

Golf Can't be this Simple

The Swing

John Toepel, Jr.
Fairway Press

Illustrations by   Alex Powers
Invaluable assistance by.....Frank Williams

Concept Golf…the game within you

Golf Can't
be this
Simple

The Swing

A revolutionary teaching approach
that makes golf fun

Published by:
Fairway Press
Wake Forest, NC
1-919-570-9772
www.conceptgolf.com

Printed in the United States of America

ISBN
0-9719208-0-X

Acknowledgments

Concept Golf is a discovery, not an invention. It is a discovery of the truths that have always existed. These truths have one source, God.

Linda is my wife and friend. She always encourages me, especially with Concept Golf.

Frank Williams has given invaluable assistance in writing this book and the growth of Concept Golf with his public relations and marketing skills.

Eric Morales has become a friend and business associate through Concept Golf.

Alex Powers read the manuscript and was inspired to create the artwork you see throughout the book.

Skip Lawrence continues to tell me that the world needs to know the ideas of Concept Golf. Write the book.

Jimmy Ballard introduced me to the true and complete idea of the golf swing. He gave me the total picture of the swing.

There have been hundreds of comments by players and students that have helped cause the ideas of Concept Golf. Thanks to all of you and to all of those who unknowingly helped.

Table of Contents

PART I   THE SWING

PART II   THE SHORT GAME

Welcome to Concept Golf

You are about to discover a remarkable teaching concept where learning to play golf is easy and the game is fun. Concept Golf will reveal The Game Within You. Everything you need to play the game well exists within you right now. Concept Golf will give you the knowledge and understanding you need to play well consistently and to have fun.

Introduction

As I watch students hit shots during our first hour of instruction, I often hear them make involuntary sounds of pleasure. Those sounds are the greatest music to my ears. As I watch students transformed from unhappy golfers to happy golfers in just a couple of hours, I am increasingly awed by the ideas and philosophy behind Concept Golf.

The purpose of this book is to help frustrated golfers everywhere improve their games quickly and permanently by sharing the simple, yet powerful, ideas of Concept Golf. Golf is such a beautiful game, and while it is difficult, it is not impossible. The ideas and principles outlined in this book provide a foundation of knowledge and understanding which will allow you to develop a golf swing that enables you to hit consistently good shots.

This book demanded to be written. Too many golfers give up the game out of frustration and embarrassment. Part of that frustration is a result of the traditional way golfers are taught. They are taught *what* the golf swing is, but not *how* to do it. This is not to say that golf teachers are bad people or are intentionally making the learning difficult. I simply believe there is an easier, more effective way to learn the game of golf. That is Concept Golf.

The lessons I had when I was playing on the PGA Tour never really solved my problems. They were always given on the driving range, and the goal was to "fix" the swing by getting my body into very specific positions during the swing. If the teacher could "fix" my swing on the range, he had "fixed" my golf game - so he thought.

During those lessons there was never any discussion about the whole idea of the swing -- only about individual pieces of the swing. Jimmy Ballard was the one teacher who finally explained the whole swing before we went to the range. **As a PGA Tour Player, I wanted the same thing you want - consistency!** The teachers didn't give me that. I knew it was possible because I played with golfers that were consistently good.

I taught the traditional way for years. Some students would improve temporarily. Others would get no better or would experience a set-back and exclaim, "I always expect to get worse after a lesson. It may take me a while to put into practice what you have taught me."

When the ideas of Concept golf began to take shape in my mind I knew that they would create a solid foundation for every student. Students who applied the Concept Golf principles quickly improved, and their improvement continued over time. Now I have the pleasure of watching previously frustrated golfers improve quickly and continue to get better.

Concept Golf has five simple swing principles or fundamentals which create the foundation for a solid golf swing. That's all. There are no more. These principles define the swing and are the cause of every desired effect. Because they are changeless ideas they are the rock upon which to build a sound swing. They answer all the questions and logically explain and define the swing.

The five principles can help you make golf fun again. They will help you become a better golfer. We will start by looking at the complete picture, the complete golf swing. Contrast this approach with traditional golf instruction in which you are taught details and specific positions you "must" use to create the swing. As you apply the Concept Golf principles, you will develop your swing based on these principles. It will look like no other golfer's swing.

The game is quite unpredictable, but your swing need not be. It should be based on clear, simple, correct principles. You shouldn't have any confusion or doubt. This book and the Concept Golf philosophy will give you that confidence.

Your coach,
John Toepel, Jr.

Part I

The Swing

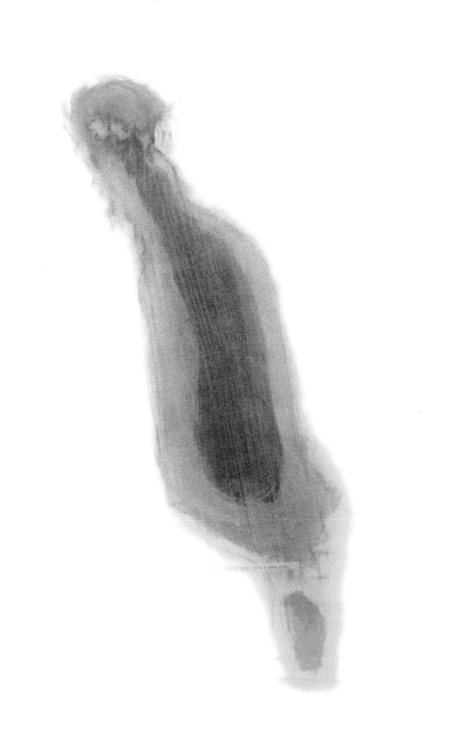

Golf Can't be this Simple - The Swing

1

This Game Called Golf

I'm going to startle you -- golf can be fun! It doesn't always have to be frustrating and embarrassing. I'm going to further startle you by telling you that learning the golf swing can be easy and painless. These statements are certainly contrary to the experience of most golfers, but they are true. Let's start your journey into the enjoyable game of golf.

Golf is the greatest game ever devised. It is completely irrational, unexplainable and has the potential to be more fun than marbles. It is played on a beautiful countryside in a quiet setting and usually with great people. It yields some of our greatest joy and greatest disappointments.

There are only two reasons to keep playing golf. One is because you played so well yesterday that you can't wait to play well again today. The other is that you played so poorly yesterday that you can't wait to play today and prove to yourself that you are a much better player than you showed yesterday.

Actually, there is a third reason, the sheer beauty of the course. Pebble Beach has to be one of the prettiest places on earth.

Golf seems to be a very complex game that taps all of your resources if you are to play reasonably well. *It has been defined as an ineffectual endeavor to put an insignificant pellet into an obscure hole with entirely inadequate weapons.*

The reality is that the game is very simple: Hit the ball with the stick until it goes in the hole 18 times. *It does become a bit more challenging when you make the decision to keep score.*

Isn't it rather silly to be working so hard to get a 1.68-inch diameter ball into a 4.25-inch diameter hole in the ground? Imagine this: If you're good at it, you will be paid millions and become famous.

Early golf courses in the US were built without a practice range. Who would ever "practice" this game? It was a game to be *played*, and no one ever expected that some fools would actually practice. How things have changed!!

The challenge of the game has made some people want to master it. Golfers now practice more than they play and have not only built exotic practice areas at the courses, but have built special facilities away from the courses where golfers can practice well after sundown.

In addition to abundant practice ranges, we now have high speed video, split screen imaging, comparative analysis, several hundred books, thousands of videos and The Golf Channel, all to make sure you have the exact scientific information about every inch of the swing.

No one has ever conquered the game, but a few have come closer than most. We can understand *why* they did it, but the question yet unresolved is *how* they did it. Is the magic they performed something that any golfer can have? Is it something you can have? Or is good golf only for the chosen few with special talents? Is there some way you can have some assurance the ball is going to go where you want it to go? Is it really possible to be consistent? You're filled with questions but haven't found any answers.

Volumes have been written about the golf swing, but little has been written about playing the game. The average score continues to go higher and frustration continues to rise. Why can some make this game look easy while the rest think it's the hardest game in the world?

There are answers, and this book is filled with them. You will learn a simple way to develop an effective golf swing. You will develop a greater understanding of how to play the game. You will find real answers to your questions. The ideas in this book will make it unnecessary for you to look for "quick fixes" for your game and swing. The principles which form the foundation of Concept Golf will make you a better golfer. It's happened to countless of Concept Golf students, and it will happen to you.

This may surprise you: *The swing is not as important to golf as you have been told.* It is one of the tools you need to understand and be able to use if you are to deliver the ball to your target. However, many other aspects of golf are much more important than the swing.

Because the swing, like the game, is a mystery, many golfers spend a great deal of time examining it. They are trying to figure out exactly what it is and how it works.

The scientific community has been brought in to determine exactly what it is that Ben Hogan did, what Byron Nelson did, and what Tiger Woods does. All their swings look so different and yet they have all played so well.

Concept Golf discovered the *swing principles* that create these great golfers' effective swings. These same principles are present in every good player's swing.

It would be difficult to be a good player without being a reasonably good ball striker.

The first section of this book gives you the ideas you need to develop an effective golf swing. The second section deals with the ideas that give you a great short game.

2

Concept Golf is Revolutionary

Concept Golf is a new solution to an old problem: taming the game of golf. Concept Golf is revolutionary because its approach to teaching the swing and the game are grounded in *ideas and thoughts* which impact your body's movements. You don't need to try to change your swing or even think about what your body is doing. The changes in your swing take place as your understanding of the swing changes, **without conscious effort.**

I am still curious as to why golfers think they need an instruction manual on how to make a swing.

Use your legs to make the swing

Concept Golf takes a revolutionary look at golf and the golf swing. This is not just theory; it is based on my experience as a PGA Tour Player, the instruction I received from several of the best teachers in the world, over 25 years of experience teaching golf, and a lot of inspiration. It is not just theory. These principles have been taught to golfers of all levels with excellent results. They are now happy, consistent golfers, and they understand the swing and the game.

Conventional instruction seems, at best, to cause temporary improvement. I've witnessed Tour Players, as well as golfers of all levels, get "fixed" with conventional instruction, but not be able to maintain the improvement. After returning to the teacher for another "fix," they would improve but, again, only temporarily. The Concept Golf view of instructing golfers, in style and substance, is quite different from traditional teaching. It's different for a good reason -- it helps the golfer improve <u>permanently</u>. It creates the consistency golfers want.

Think back to your youth when the kids in the neighborhood would get together for a pick-up game of baseball. There were no coaches, umpires or parents, and the game was a *game*. No one told you how to throw the ball, how to catch the ball, or how to hit the ball. Almost immediately, you were able to throw right to the first baseman's glove. Hitting and catching "hot" grounders took

Teachers have been teaching *what* the swing is rather than *how* to make an effective swing

more time, but soon these feats were also possible. Imagine how much harder these accomplishments would have been if you had someone telling you how to hold the ball, where your right elbow "had" to be when throwing, and what you should be doing with your feet.

When you missed the first baseman's glove, *you didn't run off to take throwing lessons.* You simply kicked the ground and waited for the next chance. The goals were clear and, with practice, you learned to meet those goals.

Not everyone had the same throwing motion, batting stance, or glove. The game was about **results,** and there was no prescribed way to accomplish those results. *Today's golfers have been so bogged down in the "how to" of the process that they have lost all sense of the goal: To shoot the lowest score by hitting fairways, greens and holes.* Golfers from the Arnold Palmer era had as many swings as our town baseball team had. Today's golfers spend endless hours trying to find the "perfect swing" when, in fact, there is no such animal.

Children don't want to know how the process called the swing works. All they're interested in is hitting the target with the ball. They will develop an effective swing in a relatively short time because their goal is to hit the target, not develop a good swing or just hit the ball. Why not be like a child and let the golf swing that exists within you reveal itself, when you define your goal as hitting the ball to the target? By trying to micromanage the body into positions prescribed by "experts," you simply interfere with your system's ability to do a perfect job for you. *I encourage you to **get out of the way** and let your system work its magic and uncover the effective swing that already exists within you.* Forget the swing "laws" and "rules" and come along for a journey that will make the swing and the game as simple as it can be and make you the golfer you are capable of being.

<u>Byron Nelson's PGA Tour record in 1945:</u>

He played in 31 tournaments.
He won 18.
He won 11 in a row.
He was second in 7.
He was third in 1.
He was fourth in 1.
He was sixth in 1.
He was ninth in 1.
He had 70 consecutive rounds under 70.
His scoring average 68.33.
That scoring-average record lasted for 55 years.

Now, that's a good year!

3

Solid Foundation

There are two components to the game of golf:

1) Delivering the ball to your chosen target and

2) Knowing where to hit the ball with what kind of shot.

It's much like driving a car --being able to shift and steer (deliver the ball to a target) are necessary *tools* for every driver. However, in order to become a very good driver, one must learn *all* of the subtleties of driving on the road with other cars (knowing where to hit the ball with what kind of shot).

My job, and the goal of this book, is to make you a better golfer. Three things must occur in order for this to happen:

1) You must develop an understanding of the misconceptions and myths that are probably confusing you without your conscious knowledge;

2) I need to create a simple, clear picture of the golf swing for you; and

3) You need to understand that this newly-created narrow road is your only path for the rest of your life.

For golf to be more fun you need to build your swing on a very solid foundation. *It must be built on a rock rather than shifting sand.* The Concept Golf principles provide you with a solid foundation while the many "quick fixes" are only shifting sand.

As you come to understand these ideas you will have no more indecision, no more doubt. You will not be inclined to hit thousands of practice balls in order to find the answer. These truths build such a solid foundation that you will not be tempted to "fix" a bad shot swing. You won't want to find out what's wrong after a bad shot, a bad nine, a bad day or a bad week.

Swing tinkering is a recipe for disaster. Ian Baker-Finch, Chip Beck and hundreds of other very good golfers have tried to "fix" their swings after some poor play and it hasn't worked.

David Duval expressed a good, mature attitude for a golfer. After shooting 63 on Sunday and winning the tournament, a TV commentator asked him, "David, I understand you didn't play too well yesterday, didn't hit it too well. Did you go to the range and fix your swing?" David's answer expressed his confidence in his swing and his foundation. "No, I went home and watched a movie. My swing is fine. It just didn't work so well on Saturday."

You need a solid foundation on which to base your vision of the golf swing and the game. You need to be able to trust your swing and game plan. Learn to accept some bad shots and poor rounds experienced by all golfers.

A bit of true humor

There are two things you can learn by stopping your backswing at the top and checking the position of your hands: (1) How many hands you have, and (2) which hand is wearing the glove.

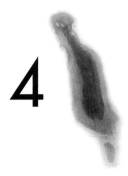

4

Misconceptions

As I've watched golfers swing and hear them talk to other golfers about their swing, it has become obvious that most of them are laboring under several wrong swing concepts -- many times unconsciously. Three of those major misconceptions are:

Misconception #1 -- <u>The swing is designed to hit the ball.</u> If that's the goal of the swing then it can be done without any training or even any aiming. Go ahead, drop a ball and grab a club and give it a whack. Nice hit. If we're just trying to hit the ball, don't finish reading this book, don't buy that new driver, and don't bother keeping score. How often do we hear people say, "If I could just hit the ball?" As we said, hitting the ball is not your goal. Your goal should be to deliver the ball to the target. For most golfers this is a big shift in their thought process. **Stop focusing on getting the head of the club on the ball and start thinking of getting the ball to the target.**

Misconception #2 -- It's up to you to get the ball in the air. You are not required to slip the club under the ball and help it up in the air. We want the ball in the air, but that's not your job or even the swing's job. It's the club's job. The loft of the club is what gets the ball in the air. **You should try to hit grounders, even if your want to hit a sand wedge straight up.** "Oh great," you say, "Here I am hitting all my shots along the ground and you are telling me to try to hit grounders. I'm doing that. Tell me how to get it in the air."

Again, you need to understand that it's not your job to get the ball in the air; it's the club's job. This is one of the major misconceptions held by golfers today. As they consciously attempt to create a swing that will get the ball up in the air, they hit behind the ball and hit grounders.

Misconception #3 -- The greatest misconception of all is that great physical effort produces a very long shot. Hitting the ball a long way is very satisfying. Since the green is 180 yards away, you naturally think in terms of force to get the ball to go that far. Our instincts tell us that the harder we swing, the further the ball will go. The more we think of swinging hard, the more we tend to swing the club with great effort from the arms and shoulders. That kind of swing creates muscular tension in the shoulders. Tension slows the arms, and thus the club, to their slowest possible speed. An effective swing is one that seems very effortless. It's always a surprise to see the ball go so far with such an effortless swing. Once I help you overcome the distance misconception, we almost will be ready to discuss the five principles, the right ideas, that will give you the solid foundation to make you a very good ball striker.

I once read a story that highlights this misconception that great physical effort produces long shots. A high-school football player had just made a tackle during a scrimmage. It was done forcefully but very awkwardly. The coach came over and said, "You should have more grace." To this young football player, grace was not what he expected to be lectured on by the coach. But he listened as the coach went on, saying "You'll find that when you are the most graceful, you'll be using the correct form and will be the most powerful. There is more power in moving with grace than with physical force." When I read that, I thought of the golfers I teach who try to use great physical force when grace would have them hit longer shots. Aren't Michael Jordan and Pete Sampras graceful? Aren't they also effective? The same applies to your golf swing.

Once you have overcome the misconception that great physical effort produces very long shots, we will be ready to discuss the five principles. The principles will give you the solid foundation you are looking for to become a good ball striker.

Those are the three major misconceptions that give many golfers problems. With this knowledge and understanding you will avoid them.

Did you know?

There are five golfers who have won all four professional Major golf championships.

They are Gene Sarazen, Ben Hogan, Jack Nicklaus, Gary Player and Tiger Woods.

5

Thought Produces Motion

Although we are talking about the swing at this point, we are doing so with the intention of you learning the swing through these "big ideas," *then forgetting all about the swing and just playing golf.* The goal is for you to learn the tool in order to play the game, then give up continually trying to "fix" the tool. Neither the swing nor the game can be perfected. Learning to accept some not-so-perfect shots is part of learning how you can best play the game.

Your golf swing is the expression of your thoughts. The only way to correctly create or change your swing is to alter

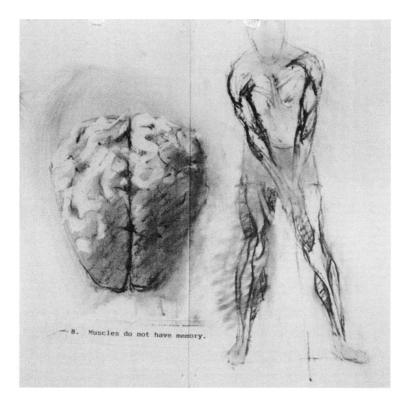

8. Muscles do not have memory.

There is no "muscle memory." Muscles do not have memory.

your thinking and understanding of the swing. Think about that! Manipulating the body into specific positions will have, at best, a very temporary effect on your swing and ball striking ability. The effect may be positive, but in many cases it is negative. **Effective, permanent changes to your swing must first occur in your thoughts.** Your body responds to your thinking - but your thinking will not respond to the positions of the body.

Thoughts are changeless, while contrived body positions have no permanence. It makes good sense to address your thoughts rather than asking you to feel the pressure of the little finger of the left hand at the top of the backswing, with a driver on the first tee of a member-guest tournament. We are going to discuss ideas that will create a swing that works for you.

Do you question whether your thinking *can really control your swing?* Just remember what happens on the first tee with your friends watching. It is not the same swing as on the range, is it? (By the way, don't worry about the first tee jitters; it happens to the Tour Players.) How do you feel about the shot over the lake for all the money? Are you as relaxed as with a practice swing? Even a two-foot putt for the best round of your life might have you making a different stroke.

It makes sense to work on the cause of the desired effects of your swing (your thinking) rather than attempting

Conscious micro-management of the body during the swing does not work

to fix the *effects* by forcing your body into specific, "necessary" positions. This idea forms the basis of the Concept Golf philosophy. This should come as a great relief if you have been following all the "rules" and haven't improved.

To make your body get into a new position through the micro-management style you must "feel" the new position. Just a quick note about "feeling" the swing and the position changes: It is unreliable for you to try to "feel" new positions because that is a very inexact sense at best. It is unreliable because it changes from moment to moment, from person to person. If you have the "feel" today and try to recapture that same "feel" tomorrow, you probably will need to over-do the movement to get the same "feel." Usually you will create major swing problems by overdoing the move that created yesterday's "feel." Did you ever try to shorten your backswing? You make what you think is a half swing and your "teachers" (your three friends) say you shortened it about an inch. "Feel" is very deceptive.

Concept Golf is a different approach that may have you a little uneasy at first. However, if you have tried the "micro-management-of-the-body" theory you probably have not improved, and actually may have had higher scores. You need to give the Concept Golf ideas a good try. Rather than doing things the same way and expecting different results, try the revolutionary ideas of Concept Golf and get good results.

To get better, you need to focus on the big ideas and the principles that are the bedrock ideas of this mysterious motion we affectionately call the golf swing.

Byron Nelson's PGA Tour record in 1944

He won 10 tournaments.
He was second in 6.
He was third in 5.
He was fourth in 1.
He was sixth in 2.

It appears he was just warming up for 1945.

Make yourself *arm-less* during the swing

6

The Golf Swing

The way golfers talk about the swing, you might get the impression that it is the most important part of the game. *You even may get the idea that the swing is the game itself.* Nearly everything that is written about golf tells you how to make your swing "perfect," just like some PGA Tour Player. *What is this mysterious thing called the swing and how does it work?*

Actually, the swing is <u>not</u> the most important aspect of the game of golf. It is an important <u>tool</u> which any good player should understand, but it is an *effect* rather than a *cause*. **The swing is an effect of your concept, or under standing, of the swing, combined with your idea of the**

type of shot required at the moment.

In Chapter Four we debunked some of the most prominent myths about the golf swing. Now that they are out of the way, we can begin to develop the foundation of ideas that will make you a solid golfer and a dependable ball striker. Once you clear your mind of misinformation and confusion, you will have a complete, simple, correct picture of the golf swing. This picture is the permanent foundation of your golf swing. It will not change from minute to minute or from good shot to bad shot. We are not going to ask you to try to get your left arm into a certain position, demand you hold the club in a very specific way, or impose any of a thousand specific body positions that are "required" in order to "perfect" your golf swing. **Instead, we are going to help you develop a clear understanding of the concept of the swing and thus create the correct picture in your mind.**

Your golf swing is actually a function of your thoughts. The Concept Golf principles will help you take control of the thoughts that create your golf swing. If you will take the time and exercise patience and discipline, you can develop an effective swing of your own.

When you learned how to throw a ball into a glove, you didn't throw the ball, miss the glove high and right, and then spend a lot of time carefully analyzing every minute detail of your motion in order to be more accurate with your next throw. No way! You simply threw another ball, then another and another, most of the time getting closer to your target.

With something as simple as throwing a ball to a glove, you allowed your "system" to correct your motion until you finally hit the glove. Every time you threw the ball your "system" would get information on where the ball went and unconsciously made corrections to your motion for the next throw. That's how and why you developed a good throwing motion.

You are not practicing as much as you are simply letting your system teach your body to throw more accurately. The same thing will happen in golf if you LET it. As you pick out a target and try to hit it with the ball, your "system" will develop an effective motion that will enable you to hit the target more frequently. Be patient and persistent, just like you were when you learned to throw.

When I was growing up and learning to play golf, there were several one-liners that were taught as the "essence of the correct golf swing:" "Head down," "Left arm straight," "Eye on the ball," "Turn in a barrel," "Slow back swing," "Stay behind the ball," "Watch the club hit the ball," "Never look up," "Finish," etc, etc. In spite of all we've been taught, these comments certainly do not define the essence of the golf swing. But isn't that what we've been taught for many years? With the advent of the high-tech, slow-motion video analysis equipment, this has begun to change. Now, in addition to the old set of one-line "must-haves" of a good golf swing, we've added "10,137" new "must" positions for a golf swing that will hit the ball. This amounts to little more than working with the effects -- in many cases idiosyncrasies -- of a player's swing. In reality, it has <u>nothing</u> to do with the true causes of an effective golf swing. These positions do not define the golf swing. They do not give you a vision of the big picture, of what an effective golf swing looks like. That vision of the big picture is <u>exactly</u> what you need to develop an effective swing.

The best way to start is to look at the big picture, the whole idea of the swing, not just its individual pieces. How does the whole swing work? What are the causes of an effective swing? It's much more sensible to *work from the whole to the parts*, and not the other way around. *The grip, stance and all the other parts of the swing make sense <u>when they fit into the big picture.</u>*

The whole concept of the swing is to *move the body with the legs* and *relax the shoulders*. Because the arms are attached at the shoulders, they will be moved when the body moves. When the movement of the body moves the arms, they will be moved correctly, quickly and consistently. **The arms should always *follow* the body during the backswing and the swing through the ball. The arms must be *dependent* on the body, not *independent*.**

The swing is the part of golf that gets all of the attention and all of the ink, while in reality the swing is nothing more than a simple tool of the game. It's easy to learn and easy to do. It is not something that must be done perfectly. Your swing does not have to look like Ben Hogan's swing or Fred

Couples' swing -- unless, of course, you are Fred Couples or Ben Hogan. It must be your swing based on the correct principles of an effective golf swing. **Your swing will not look like anyone else's swing, but it will be fundamentally the same as the good players' swings.** You are shorter, taller, fatter, thinner, more or less flexible etc. than everyone else, so your swing must be different and yet the same. The commonalities are found in the principles, the fundamentals, not in the mechanics.

Don't think that you must make a perfect swing and be in exactly this position or that position, in order to have a small chance to make some sort of contact with the ball. *The correct swing is a very casual, effortless motion done with the intent of moving that small, innocent ball to a target off in the distance.* If the swing feels like work, it's wrong. The hard part of golf is the playing of the game and the self-control. That's what makes this game so captivating. It always gives us a reason to come back tomorrow. We will discuss the swing, but it will be on the "you can do it" basis rather than from the "it's the toughest thing in the world" mentality. We're going to free up your thinking and get you away from the so-called "perfect body positions" that are considered "laws" of golf. *It is your thinking that makes your body move, correctly or incorrectly.* Let's get your thinking right ... the game within you.

The five Concept Golf swing principles

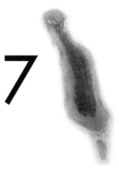

7

Where Did the Principles Come From?

How did I discover and develop the principles that form the foundation of Concept Golf? These ideas were discovered as a result of my experience, including playing on the PGA Tour for five years, teaching golfers for over 25 years, and a great deal of thought and inspiration. The realization and understanding that all athletics utilize the same basic athletic motion was thrown into the mix as I discovered these revolutionary principles.

I had the opportunity to learn from some of the best teachers in the world, and some of these ideas came from them. My teachers include Jimmy Ballard, Johnny Revolta, Jim Flick, Phil Rogers and Norman von Nida in Australia. I must point out that the only teacher who explained the big picture of the swing before we actually went to work on my swing, was Jimmy Ballard.

Playing competitive golf with the best players in the world was a great experience and quite an education. Some of my "playmates" included Jack Nicklaus, Gary Player, Tom Watson, Ray Floyd, J. C. Snead, Bruce Fleisher, Tom Kite, and many other Tour Players. My experience playing at this level and with these top-flight players has provided me with knowledge and insight that can help you become a better golfer.

Part of Concept Golf's insight into the swing is rooted in the understanding that there is **one basic athletic motion which is used in all of athletics.** The golf swing is golf's version of this athletic motion. It is the same basic motion that is used to hit a tennis ball, throw a football, kick a soccer ball, or break a rack in pool.

To describe the athletic motion, let's take a look at the baseball pitcher. Why the pitcher? You are familiar with the pitching motion and have probably thrown a ball or two yourself. The pitcher does what you as a golfer want to do; throw it fast, accurately and consistently. As a golfer you want to hit it far and down the middle with consistency.

So just how does the pitcher throw the ball? How do you throw a ball? It's not complicated. Let's take a look so we can apply these principles to the golf swing. After getting the sign from the catcher, the pitcher begins his wind-up by moving his body so that all of his weight is on his back foot, the one on the pitching rubber. By doing this, he has caused the arm to be flung away, in the direction opposite from where he will deliver the ball. When all the weight is on the back leg *and the arm is still going away from the target,* he reverses the direction of the body by pushing off his back foot. This causes his body to be pushed toward the target.

The arm was still going away when the body changed directions. The arm only changes directions when it can go no further back and is pulled swiftly toward the target by the forward motion of the body. This allows the arm to function with maximum effectiveness, speed, and accuracy. The arm is completely *dependent* on the body. The arm moves ONLY because the body moves it, not because the muscles of the arm made the arm move.

Have you ever seen a major league pitcher stand flat-footed and pitch the ball? Of course not; any pitcher knows that he will have neither speed nor accuracy if he throws the ball flat-footed. To be effective he must use the big muscles (the legs and back muscles) to move the body in order to create speed and accuracy necessary for a good throw.

I want you to try to throw the ball as far as you can, but with different rules. In order to be very powerful, you must hold the ball as tightly as possible, tightening all the muscles in your arm and shoulder. I want to see all the veins popping out; that way I know you are powerful and can throw it far. *You know instinctively as you tighten up or quit moving the body, you can't throw the ball any distance at all.*

I regularly see golfers holding the club so tightly and flexing those shoulder muscles, and then wondering why they can't hit the ball far. Great muscular effort doesn't work.

For confirmation, tighten up your arms and take a practice swing. Listen for any noise the club makes. There's not much air moving, is there? Now try again, but with your arms completely relaxed. Listen for the loud noise of the club through the air. Quite a difference, right?

In order to have the arms and shoulders move at their top possible speed and reliability, they must be kept relaxed. This is achieved when the legs, which are the body's real source of strength, cause the arms and shoulders to move.

Simply stated, the feet and legs cause the trunk of the body to move, which in turn causes the arms to move. All types of athletics are played with the feet moving the body. It all comes from the ground up, never from the top down. For an observation, watch someone throw a bowling ball or throw a horseshoe to a post. The legs move the body, and the arm is completely dependent upon them. It's the same in all of athletics, including golf.

Because we are holding this long stick with the intention of ending this little, innocent ball's very life, this is contrary to our golf instincts. Common sense would tell us that in order to end that poor little ball's life, (without missing the ball, of course), we must use those powerful arms - and never look up? Isn't that right? **Not so!**

There you have it -- the process through which I developed the Concept Golf swing principles that will take your golf game to a new level. Because these ideas are simple, and because there are only five fundamentals, you might be tempted to not give them proper reverence. These principles have been tested and proven by golfers just like you. The new golfer, the professional, the high handicapper and the plus-one handicapper have all profited from these few simple ideas. The Concept Golf swing principles are simple, logical, easy to understand, and easy to put into action. Everything else in the golf swing is a result of these few fundamentals -- for all clubs, for all shots. They apply to the full swing, the short wedge and even the putter. As you understand and accept these ideas and put them to use, you will see great progress in your golf game.

8

Introducing the Five Principles

If you emulate the baseball pitcher's motion in your golf swing, your swing will be strong, accurate and consistent. Follow the pitcher's lead.

There are five principles which form the foundation of a good golf swing -- no more, no less. Principles are fundamental truths. **These principles are the same for all golfers** -- Jack Nicklaus, John Toepel, Andrea Toepel, Joe Slugger, or Alice Brushthegrass.

Principles don't change. These principles are the same today, yesterday and 10,000 years hence. In addition, **these principles are the cause of every effect.** The Concept Golf principles are the fundamentals which undergird an effective golf swing. They are all-inclusive and cause every positive effect of the swing. They are everything you must *understand* in order to have an effective swing. When you have a correct *understanding* of these principles and incorporate them into your swing, all the positive effects you want will fall into place. It should be a great relief to find out that there are only five things you need to learn and understand in order to improve your golf game. Most of the golfers I teach arrive with so many scattered thoughts, so many "necessary positions" they believe they must assume, and so many conflicting views of the swing that they are in a constant state of paralyzed confusion.

The Concept Golf principles will eliminate that state of confusion. Less is better. The less information you are confronted with, the clearer your thinking will be and the easier it is for you to have a good swing and hit good shots.

The five principles are divided into two categories: Two static and three dynamic principles. The static principles are ideas you need to understand *before* you swing, while the dynamic principles are inclusive ideas that will create your effective golf swing.

The Static Principles

(1) The **address position** is a good athletic position that will allow you to make a powerful swing consistently.

(2) Once you have assumed a strong address position, **align** the club and the body so the swing can be efficient and effective.

The Dynamic Principles

The foundation idea, the one that makes all the others possible, is simple **(3) weight transfer**: the moving of the body so it can function efficiently with little effort. Once your weight is being properly transfered, we can discuss the concept of **(4) shoulder relaxation.**

Lastly, you need to understand the function and position of the **(5) right leg and knee** which is the source of your power.

That's it. These are the five principles you need to know and be able to implement in order to become a better ball striker. The greater your understanding of these ideas, the better ball striker you will be.

Now we'll discuss these ideas in greater detail and I'll explain how to incorporate them in your swing. Learning the swing should be a matter of a few hours, not a lifetime. While becoming very good at the swing and the principles may take a little longer, it should not take a lifetime to develop a good, workable swing.

The five principles will take care of everything that is involved in the golf swing. That's a big statement, but these are the fundamentals of the swing, the real causes of every positive effect. You will realize quick, marked improvement in your ability to hit good shots. As you develop a greater understanding of these changeless ideas, your ball striking will continue to improve.

9

Address Position

The address position starts with the feet, which are the most important body parts in terms of the swing. Begin by spreading your feet until the inside of your heels are shoulder width apart. This stance feels wide to most golfers, so let's examine why it's important.

Let's take a look at other athletes. Pete Sampras positions himself with his feet far apart and bent forward in preparation to receive a serve. Michael Jordan has his feet far apart when he guards a player on the basketball court. A shortstop has his feet spread when a batter is at the plate. Why do these athletes have their feet spread far apart?

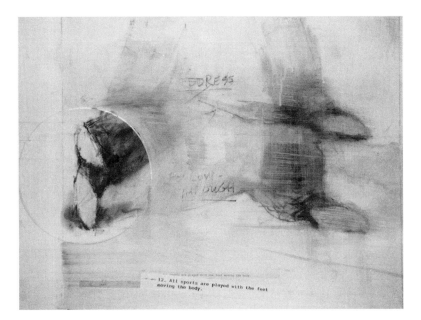

The athletic motion is made with the feet

Simply to position themselves so they can move right or left very quickly if necessary. With their feet spread far apart, they can use their legs to move the body quickly. *Athletes move their bodies with the inside front part of their feet.* The pitcher uses the front inside part of the back foot to propel his body forward very quickly so that the arm will be dragged forward quickly. The feet are the fuel of the engine;

the engine is the right leg. Keep your feet far enough apart so they can do their job efficiently and effectively.

Now you simply flex your knees and pull them slightly together and the legs are ready to work.

Next, hold the club out in front of you with the head of the club slightly above the handle. Relax your arms and bend them at the elbows. With the bottom line of the club perpendicular to the target line, put your hands on the grip of the club. *Put your hands on the grip any way you want, any way that seems right to you. There is no "right" way you "must" hold the club.*

You can overlap, interlock, use a baseball grip or hold the club cross-handed. Cross-handed? Yes, I played with Charlie Owens on the Tour and he played cross-handed and could hit it long and score low. It sounds blasphemous to be treating the grip so lightly when most teachers spend a great deal of time on getting your hand on the club exactly "right."

The grip is **not** a fundamental. It is different for every golfer. It **must** be different for every golfer. The grip must fit **your** swing, not someone else's idea of the perfect grip. Hogan's grip worked for Hogan. Couples' grip is very strong and works for him and Lietzkes' grip is weak and works for him. **There is no single grip configuration that works for all golfers.**

Hold the club **gently firm**, and that's that. Not too tight, not too loose. That's all you need to know about the grip.

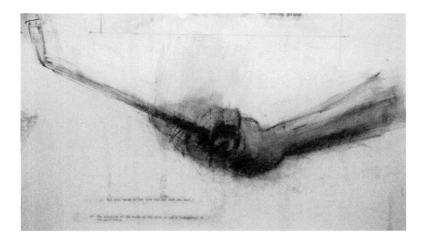

The grip is not a fundamental

Next, bend forward without tucking your chin into your chest. Keep your chin up. As you do this, let your arms unfold and set the club on the ground. It will touch the ground in exactly the right spot. It will measure the distance from the body that the ball should be placed in relation to your feet. You will find that the ball will be positioned just slightly closer to the left foot than the right foot for all clubs most of the time. It's that simple, so don't complicate it or try to make it scientific.

You are now in a *strong athletic* position. From this position you can make an athletic motion that will be simple, effective and consistent. This position allows your legs to be in charge of your body and swing. Your arms can relax and you can hit the ball as far as possible. This is one of the five swing principles of Concept Golf. Do it well.

<u>Byron Nelson's PGA Tour record in 1946</u>

He played in 21 tournaments.
He won 6.
He was second in 3.
He was third in 3.
He was fifth in 1.
He was sixth in 1.
He was seventh in 2.
He was ninth in 1.
He was thirteenth in 1.

This guy was good!

10

Alignment

Alignment is the simple positioning of the club and body so the ball can be delivered to the target with an uncomplicated swing. This is simple and important but it is often overlooked or misunderstood. To consistently hit the ball toward the target, the club and body need to be positioned correctly.

Alignment involves making an imaginary straight line through the ball to the target and simply setting the club behind the ball so that the bottom line of the club is perpendicular to the target line.

Once the club is positioned correctly, you need to position the body so that it can function most effectively. The line through your toes needs to be aimed *at least parallel* to the target line, *preferably* to the <u>left</u> of the target line (See illustration 1). With your body thus aimed, you are able to make a swing that will have the club on line to the target throughout the entire swing.

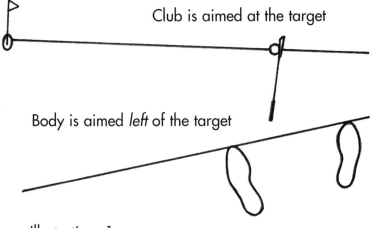

Club is aimed at the target

Body is aimed *left* of the target

Illustration 1

What happens if your body is **not** aimed to the left of your target? Most of the golfers that come to me for instruction are inclined to aim their body at the target or even to the right of the target (See illustration 2). By this I mean that the line through the tips of their toes tends to point toward the target or to the right of the target. For some reason golfers think that aiming their body at the target will facilitate the ball going toward the target.

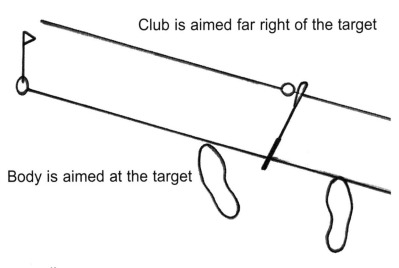

Club is aimed far right of the target

Body is aimed at the target

Illustration 2

If the body is aimed at the target, or to the right of the target, the club is actually aimed much further to the right. Such an alignment will cause the swing to redirect to an outside-in path during the downswing in hopes of getting the ball to go toward the target. It will cause a glancing blow to the ball and result in a weak shot. *Do not worry that aiming your body to the left of the target line will cause a fade or slice. That is a myth.* You can fade or draw from any alignment.

Alignment can be easily demonstrated by placing two golf balls about 3 feet apart, one is the target and the other is the golfer's ball. The target line is most obvious when the two golf balls are close together. You can easily set the golf club perpendicular to that imaginary line. Next, simply position your body so that the line through your toes is either parallel to the target line, preferably aiming at a point to the left of the target. Now you are in position to make a swing during which the club stays on the line to the target, or in golf vernacular, *on the plane*. A straight, solid shot at your target will be your consistent result.

However, if you position your body with the line through your toes aiming at the target, you can see how far to the right of the target the golf club is actually aimed. (See illustration 2). If the golf club is aimed way to the right of the target, your body will make a compensating move during the downswing to try to get the ball to go toward the target. This creates the outside-in swing that will result in weak, unreliable shots.

Golfers who aim to the right have a standard shot: a miss-hit which consistently slices. I witnessed a US Open champion playing in a Senior Tour event. He was aiming far to the right. I watched him hit two shots with irons, the first of which was a miss hit that went way to the right of the target. The second was almost a grounder. Good alignment allows your body and system to create a swing that will consistently deliver the object to the target. This is deceptively important and simple. It's easy to get it right and causes mountains of trouble if you get it wrong.

I have instructed many students who were having a great deal of difficulty striking the ball because of faulty alignment. Once they understood and utilized proper alignment, their ball striking immediately improved and they were able to enjoy the game once again.

I also remember watching Tom Kite practice. He always practiced with a club on the ground to make sure his alignment was correct. If you want to put a club on the ground to check your alignment, put it six inches outside the ball on the line aimed at the target. Let your feet go to the left of that line but don't put a club along your toes (See illustration 3).

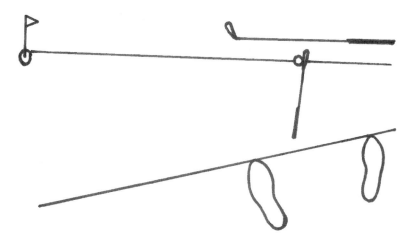

Illustration 3

Alignment is important and simple. It takes place before you swing. Please understand it and get it right now or you will forever lose power, accuracy, low scores, good caddies and the club championship.

Align to the target, not the golf ball. I see many high handicappers working hard to get in a good address position at the golf ball, but only taking a cursory look at the target. On the other hand, good players set up to the target with a vague awareness of the golf ball being on the ground. *If you want to improve your golf game, spend a lot of time looking at the target and only a little time at the golf ball.*

Now, let's move on to the dynamic principles.

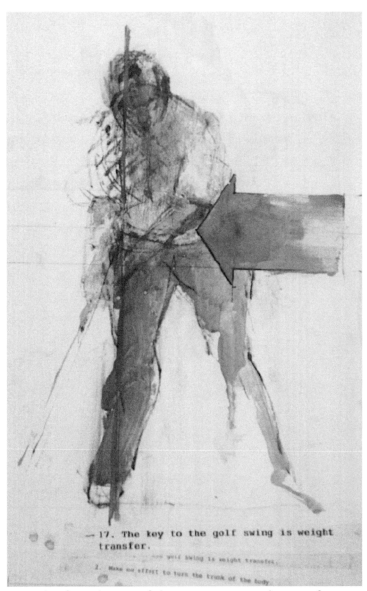

—17. The key to the golf swing is weight transfer.

The foundation of the swing is weight transfer

11

Weight Transfer

Weight transfer is the foundation of the entire swing motion. Without proper weight transfer, nothing else in your entire swing will work properly! This is the foundation upon which the whole golf swing is built. If the foundation of your swing is made of quicksand -- such as several hundred so-called "perfect" positions in which you must hold your body -- a slight shift in the wind will cause the entire swing to crumble. If your swing is built on a rock-solid foundation comprised of sound, fundamental ideas, you can withstand all that the world throws at you and still hit good shots.

The great players have that solid foundation. Nicklaus, Hogan, Nelson and a few others have that unshakable underpinning that they can't be talked out of. When the principles of the swing make sense and work, it is very unlikely that you will try to "fix" your swing because of a few bad shots -- or even a few bad weeks.

Weight transfer is simply the moving of the body's weight to the right foot and then back the left foot. The baseball pitcher moves his weight to the back foot and then to the front foot in order to utilize the strength of his body and his legs in moving his body around. In the same way, you must use the strength of your body to move your body around. You use your legs to cause the trunk of your body to move, which in turn causes your arms to be moved so that they don't have to move themselves.

Virtually all athletic motions are based on the legs using the feet to move the body. Once again, consider the earlier example of the pitcher throwing the ball. What does he use to cause the body to move? He uses his legs, through his feet. The ground provides the resistance for the feet so that the legs can do all of the work. The arm does not move itself in order for the pitcher or the golfer to be effective.

Without proper weight transfer the other principles are meaningless. The whole purpose of having the feet and legs move the body is to keep the arms relaxed and allow them to have maximum speed and consistency, returning the club through the ball for a true shot. *Most bad shots are a result of the arms trying to do all of the work.*

If the arms try to work independently of the body and move themselves, the muscles will tighten and thus move more slowly. When the arms tighten, the immediate result is a real loss of club speed, which results in poor shots. Very frequently the club will hit the ground before it can get to the ball.

For good, consistent shots the arms must be followers, not independent leaders. The arms can (and will) follow the body effectively because they are attached at the shoulders. They will be swung along the path through the ball to the target. Weight transfer is a simple concept: weight to the right, weight to the left. When working with students, I have them assume a good address position, then simply pick up the left foot, followed by the right foot in order to understand the concept and the rhythm of the weight transfer motion. One hundred percent of your weight goes to the right foot, and then one hundred percent to the left foot. This creates the swing; the arms simply follow.

Some will say that the problem is that the head is moving with the body and not staying perfectly still. Now, that is a real problem -- especially for Curtis Strange, a back-to-back US Open winner. He has a very generous lateral movement of his whole body to the right. We've been told that the head MUST stay perfectly still during the swing or you will miss the ball. Or worse than that, your buddies will say, "You looked up." I think we have been taught this "Myth of The Still Head" because the good ball striker "felt" like his head didn't move when he swung. This myth started before the advent of movie cameras and it became a "law" that the camera could not undo. People tend to accept what they are told as truth, not what actually takes place. We have accepted the myth of a perfectly still head because it has been told to us many times. However, it is not true and never has been -- so feel free to move your head with your body as your body moves to the right and to the left. NEVER try to keep your head still; it will ruin your whole swing.

Proper weight transfer is a pure lateral movement to the right and then to the left. *It's a very simple motion with no attempt to turn.* Don't try to turn the body, just move your weight over to the right foot and then over to the left foot, keeping the front of your body facing the ball. Some of you may ask, "That's just fine, but don't I have to try to turn?" I would say, "No." Most golfers think of a turn as the whole body (the shoulders and the hips) turning. The shoulders will rotate without you consciously attempting to make them turn. There are a couple of reasons you don't want the hips to turn.

The "coiling" (creating greater strength) of the body comes when there is resistance. The shoulders rotate but the hips and lower body resist and the body gets stronger. You want the hips to remain facing forward so that the right leg and foot can stay in a position of strength. If the hips turn, they will pull the right foot out of position and put your weight and pressure on the outside of your heel, rather than keeping it on the inside front part of your right foot. You cannot throw a ball with any speed or power if your weight is on the outside of your right foot; it deadens the lower body. Try throwing a ball and getting your weight to the outside of your right foot. You have no power. You don't want to try to turn the entire body; just let the shoulders rotate.

Since proper weight transfer is so important, how do you begin? Stand as if you were having a conversation, but with your feet spread shoulder-width inside your heels. Next, simply pick your left foot up in the air. Notice how all of your weight goes to your right foot. Now lift up your right foot. Notice how all your weight goes to the left foot. It's not overly complex, but it is very effective. That's all there really is to the weight transfer principle. Stand on the right foot, then stand on the left foot -- without any attempt to turn.

If you are still convinced that weight transfer is not for you because it breaks too many "rules," let's examine a swing with the body turning, and a swing that uses the proper lateral motion of weight transfer. With the "turn swing," the swing is made with a conscious effort to turn in one spot, while keeping the head still. Notice the path where the club travels with that type of swing. It goes inside very quickly and returns to the ball, then back to the inside very quickly (See illustration 4). It is on line to the target for only a moment.

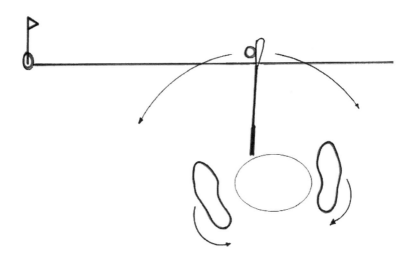

Illustration 4

It also makes you have a reverse weight shift: weight to the left then to the right. A reverse weight shift is a "power robber" and has the club on the line to the target for a very short time.

On the other hand, proper weight transfer makes you powerful and will keep the club on the target line a long time. This works (See illustration 5).

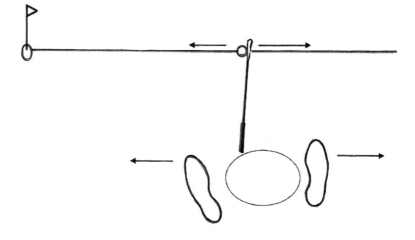

Illustration 5

No tension here

12

Relaxation

Complete relaxation in your shoulders during the swing is your key to long, straight shots. Your arms can move at their greatest possible speed only when your shoulders are completely relaxed. Proper weight transfer allows for *complete* relaxation.

With your body moving to the right foot and then back to the left foot, your legs are doing the work. Your feet and legs create the movement of the trunk of your body. The arms are attached at the shoulders, so now you can relax your shoulders and arms and they will follow the body (just as with the baseball pitcher).

The pitcher's arm must be relaxed to be in this position

The muscles in your arms never help your arms move in an effective athletic motion. They are always relaxed followers. To get an idea of how much relaxation you need, bend forward and let your arms hang until it feels as though your arms are falling out of their sockets. All the muscles around your shoulder joints must be *completely* relaxed.

Now, address the ball and let your shoulders go completely limp. Please take note here that I am not talking about relaxing your hands. You can hold the club gently firm in your hands and still keep your shoulders completely relaxed. Occasionally students will relax their grip to the point their hands will come off the club during the swing. Overly relaxed hands do not create relaxed shoulders.

For the club to move as quickly as possible, your arms must be followers of the body. It's exactly the same as when you throw a ball or make a tennis stroke. For maximum club speed and consistency, your shoulders must be completely relaxed throughout the entire swing. Complete shoulder relaxation is critical as you reverse the swing from the backswing to the swing through the ball. *If your shoulders tighten as you start the downswing, you have just caused a great loss of power and have most likely caused a poor shot.*

I usually get lots of questions at this point about whether this relaxed-shoulder swing actually works. "With my shoulders this relaxed, how do I make a backswing?" "How do I even start the backswing?" "I feel that I am losing control of the club and the swing." "I can't get any power this way. "There's no way for the club to get back to the ball and for the face to be square at impact." "How do I get on the right plane?" "This feels funny, don't I look stupid?" and so on.

How can you possibly make a backswing with such relaxed shoulders? Most golfers are used to calling it the "take-away" rather than a back swing. "Take-away" describes a manipulated motion that would force the arms to take the club to some specified spot. This creates tense and independent arms rather than arms that are relaxed because they are dependent on the moving body for their movement. A backswing with relaxed shoulders (as opposed to a "take-away") is likely to be a big change in your concept of the swing.

It is important that you understand what the backswing is and how it is created. The golfer's backswing and the baseball pitcher's windup are the same motion. The pitcher doesn't use the muscles of his arm to make his arm go to the right spot during the wind-up. He uses the motion of the body to cause the arm to be swung away.

The golfer's backswing is truly a swinging motion away from the ball. You need to be relaxed in the shoulders to let the motion of the body cause the arms to be flung away. Because your shoulders are completely relaxed, something other than the arms must cause the backswing. Creating the backswing is the job of the feet and legs. As you transfer your weight to your right foot, your body moves to the right and your arms will be dragged along. As you move more quickly to the right, the club and arms will be flung or swung to the top of the backswing in exactly the right plane and perfect position without you thinking about it or trying consciously to create it with the arms. This is the "one-piece" backswing that we hear so much about. Interesting, isn't it? The arms are made to move when the body moves.

Complete shoulder relaxation may give you the sense that the club and arms are out of control. You may feel like the club and arms are going wherever they want and like you have no chance to deliver the club to the ball. Your sense of having no control of the club or swing is correct -- and is exactly as it should be!

If you sense that you are in control of the club and your swing, you are in control of the wrong thing. *You never want to feel like you have control of the club or the swing.* If that is the case, you have lost control of the shot. It does require trust to simply allow the club and arms to go where they want. When you relax and allow the arms and club to follow their natural path your swing will improve dramatically.

You don't consciously control your arm when you throw a ball to a target; it moves freely and naturally. When you accept the concept of relaxation and trust that your arms will move correctly when they swing freely, you will quit trying to control the club or the swing. In an attempt to control the shot, golfers often grab the club tightly, creating a swing that only a mother could love. The more relaxed you get with your arms and shoulders during the whole swing, the longer and straighter you will hit shots. I promise!!

If you have any doubt about the effectiveness of relaxation, pick up a ball and prepare to throw it as far as possible. In order to throw it a long way and control where it goes, tighten your grip and shoulder. Now you are set to throw it far and accurately, right? Not a chance! You have no chance to throw it anywhere but short and crooked. Now try the same exercise with a club. Hold the club tightly and tighten your shoulders before you swing. Can you create maximum club speed with that tightness? The answer is no... tension is obviously not good for your swing.

Practice this relaxed swing at home, out of sight of your friends, until you get a sense that this swing is all right and you really don't look ridiculous. You may want to videotape a few swings at this time so that you can see yourself making a good-looking swing even though it "feels" so out of control.

One of the big misconceptions is that a relaxed swing will not hit the ball as far as you want. Distance is one of the most important aspects of a good golf game. It's important for scoring and the enjoyment of the game. With a relaxed swing, you feel like you've lost any chance to hit 300 yard drives. While nothing could be further from the truth, your instincts tell you otherwise. Proper relaxation will allow you to finally create effortless power rather than the powerless effort you are used to. You will start hitting shots further with much less effort.

How do you incorporate this shoulder relaxation into your swing? Start with the seven iron and hit some seventy-five yard shots with your body moving through weight transfer and your shoulders relaxed. This will be a pleasant experience. Gradually make the swing bigger and quicker, but never force the distance. Let the greater distance come as a result of relaxation and movement. The distance will come, and you will be surprised at how effortlessly you swing to create the distance.

The only way to consistently hit the ball on the sweet spot, with the clubface aimed at the target, is through complete shoulder relaxation. If you try to make the club hit ball on the sweet spot and make the clubface point at the target, you will hit poor shots. You can no more direct the clubface to the ball, than you can direct the baseball to the catcher's glove. Give up this notion of control; it certainly doesn't apply to the golf swing or to the playing of the game. Trying to control every aspect of your swing is like trying to control a handful of mercury. To be most effective, aim at the target and swing - then watch the ball go to the target.

One of the important by-products of relaxing your shoulders is that your hands will be leading the club head at impact and into the finish. Your hands must be in this

The hands should be well ahead of the clubhead at impact

position for good ball striking. The club head *never* passes the hands in any good golf shot. The "hands-ahead-of-the club-head" effect is not something that can be produced by control, physical effort or restriction. This effect can only be the result of complete shoulder relaxation.

Each of the five Concept Golf swing principles is very important. The concept of relaxation seems to be a challenge for some golfers, but it is a necessity and you can do it. One of the ways to have a better understanding of this concept is to make an overhand throwing motion as if you are throwing a baseball. Notice how relaxed your shoulder must be as you throw the ball. This little exercise is a good way to get a better idea of the complete shoulder relaxation that is necessary in your shoulders for throwing a ball and for the the golf swing.

Tension is the result of an incorrect concept of the swing and game. It is frequently caused by trying to force distance. Tension is also the effect of fear and self-imposed pressure. Did you ever watch the Tour Players play the last few holes in a tournament they were leading? What are they doing?

Fuzzy Zoeller is talking continuously. Some are whistling. Others are doing whatever they do to relax under this kind of self-imposed pressure. The point is that they know they must stay relaxed if they are to maintain peak performance and not allow mental tension to create physical tension.

Here is an idea to help with the mental part of this very important relaxation concept: Keep the shot and the game in the proper perspective. Stand over every shot and, just before you start your backswing, say to yourself, "So what, big deal. This is a *game* and I am having fun." Talk yourself out of the idea that this is the most important shot of your life. If your self-talk is, "Please, stay out of the water," you're creating tension. Lighten up and give yourself a chance to succeed! Get the attitude that you're a disinterested observer, nothing more. Relax your thoughts and watch your shoulders relax. Relaxation is an important principle. Here's a true story that further highlights its value.

Some time ago, I was playing golf in Hilton Head with a friend and student, Tommy Arnold. As we warmed up, I watched Tommy hit a few shots. When we had played the previous day, Tommy had hit several tee shots far to the right. He was concerned and I wanted to help him find a solution.

I could see him really working over every shot. I noticed his face was all screwed up as he got ready to make the swing. He looked like he had just gotten a bad financial report and was sucking on a lemon.

I asked him if I might make a suggestion and he said, "Of course." I told him to relax his face until his lips "fell off" during his swing preparation. I'm sure he thought I was going to tell him how to reposition his hands or some other mechanical adjustment to keep from hitting it to the right.

As he relaxed his face and his lips "slid to the ground," his swing smoothed out and his ball striking improved greatly. He thought the lesson was a bit strange, but he liked the improvements to his game. You can't be sad and sing a happy song. Neither can you have a relaxed face and a tense body. Tension was causing his arms to be tight as he swung through the ball, and this made his shots go to the right.

As I teach golfers this principle, they often give an involuntary exclamation of joy and amazement after their first good golf shot. The swing was so effortless, and the ball went so far, that they couldn't help making a little whistle or a wow. That makes it all worth it to me.

Another by-product of shoulder relaxation is overcoming the *biggest power leak in the golf swing. When the arms start down before the legs and body reverse their direction, the potential power of the body is gone.* Try throwing a ball without moving the body and see how much power you have. Shoulder relaxation makes the arms wait for the body to move, and this causes the arms to be dragged through the ball with the greatest possible speed. Relax!

The flexed right leg creates a solid foundation

13

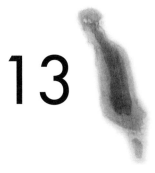

Right Leg

How do baseball pitchers create 95-mile-per-hour pitches that hit a spot the size of a grapefruit? They use the strongest part of their body, the legs, to move the body. More specifically, they use their back leg (the one on the pitching rubber). By pushing with this leg, they create the quick movement in their body that causes the arm to be moved with great enough speed to throw the ball at 95 miles-per-hour and deliver the ball to the center of the catcher's glove.

Just as the pitcher uses his back leg to throw 95 mile-per-hour pitches to a very small target, you want to use your back leg to create long, accurate shots. It is your source of consistent, effortless power.

Most golfers think their source of power is those little arms. Some of you may not have small arms but they are still smaller and weaker than your legs, aren't they? You need to use your legs so that you can have an effective swing like all the good players. A nice by-product of using your legs is that you will be as fresh on the back nine as on the front nine. Your legs make your swing powerful and help you hit the ball consistently far. Let's examine how this works.

To start the swing, move your entire body weight to the right foot quickly enough to cause the arms to be flung away. When you are positioned with your weight on the front inside part of your right foot, you need to keep your leg flexed just as it was at address. At the top of the backswing, your right knee should point at the ball and should be flexed. This will keep your weight and pressure on your big toe and ball of your right foot. Now your right foot should be in position to push your body forward at any moment during the backswing.

The temptation is to allow your weight to stay on the left foot when you are trying to keep your right knee pointed at the ball during the backswing. You need to make sure your weight actually goes to your right foot when you are trying to keep the pressure on the front inside part of your right foot. The top of the backswing is the same position you are in when you wind up to throw a ball. In fact, it's a good idea to throw a ball or two just to get the idea of the position you are going to be in. Can you imagine trying to throw a ball if you let your weight stay on your left foot or get to the outside heel of your right foot? Try it! It's not possible to have any strength or power with your weight out of position.

If your right leg straightens during the backswing, it is useless. Test this idea by straightening your legs and jumping. Don't bend them, just jump with straight legs. Doesn't work at all, does it? That's why you want your right leg flexed at the top of the backswing. As you push against the ground with your big toe and ball of your right foot, your leg straightens out and pushes your body forward with great speed and power.

Your right leg creates the quickness in your body that makes your arms move with real speed. The assumption here is that you are following the relaxation principle and your shoulders are limp at the top of your back swing. All of these principles are interdependent and rely on each other for success. If your arms are working to create the downswing your right leg won't be able to do its job. Only if your shoulders are relaxed can your right leg do its work and create the speed and consistency you want. Either your arms work or your legs work, *but your legs and arms can't both work at the same time.* When your legs do the work and your arms are relaxed followers, you will hit a lot of very good shots.

— 16. I do not discuss the swing plane.

There is no need to discuss the swing plane

14

Swing Myths

Concept Golf's foundation is based upon the five principles of a good golf swing. These true, unchanging fundamentals stand in stark contrast to many of the commonly accepted myths taught through traditional golf instruction. These are the old so-called "absolutes" that have no basis in fact. They are the one-line instructions we have heard for years. To illustrate their foolishness during my schools, I will make a swing based on these points and get quite a laugh. When it is done with slight exaggeration, the ridiculousness of these one-liners becomes very obvious and humorous.

Many of these "Old Wives Tales" of the swing have come from still photos of the PGA Tour Players. We have studied these photos from every angle and "scientifically" dissected them to analyze the positions. We want to know the position into which we "must" put our bodies in order to hit shots like the pros.

The fallacy in this approach is that still photos of a motion don't tell the whole truth; they only show you a momentary piece of the puzzle. Let me illustrate with a story about a lady who had a horse that she really liked. One day she went to take photos of the horse and when she got there the horse was lying down. She began taking pictures while the horse was lying down and he began to stand up. When she got the pictures developed, one of the pictures showed the horse as if it were in a sitting position. When she showed the pictures to her friend, her friend stopped at that picture and said, "Oh, look, your horse is sitting." The owner smiled and replied, "Horses don't sit." The picture showed the horse in a sitting position, but it didn't accurately portray what really happened. The reality was that the horse was in the process of standing up.

That's the problem we get into when we analyze still photos of a movement like a golf swing. The photo tries to freeze a moment of that movement and assume that moment is truth. This false assumption forces us to make false conclusions based on that one frozen position, but the golfer is really on his way from one position to another. Any one moment in the swing is the result of the transition between the previous moment and the next moment. Still pictures of a golf swing will give you untrue and unreliable information. On a side note, I would also suggest you don't become involved in video analysis of your swing, especially when you are compared to a Tour Player. However, if you must, make sure the videos are full speed and are taken at exactly ninety-degree angles to the target line or exactly along the target line. The very best way to get a sense of a good golf swing is to attend a PGA Tour tournament. You will get to see it and hear it in person. You will also find the spirit of the game.

There are a number of myths golfers are laboring under. Let's address these myths.

"Keep your head still" - Golfers have been told thousands of times "if you move your head, you'll miss the ball." Because everyone says it, it has become a "law," and you have been trying to keep your head perfectly still at all costs. Someone forgot to tell Byron Nelson not to move his head. He held the lowest scoring average on the PGA Tour for 55 years (68.3 in 1945). He had a big dip in his swing. And Curtis Strange, who won the US Open two consecutive years, has a very generous lateral motion with his head. So does Ben Crenshaw. We could go on and on with these examples, but the point is there are lots of exceptions to this "rule." Could it be that this "rule" is incorrect?

All this "rule" does is freeze the golfer's body and keep him from moving his body as he should. When you try to keep your head still, your body sways; that is, the hips move out from under the upper body and cause a reverse weight shift. A reverse weight shift involves your weight going to the left foot during the back swing rather than the right foot. You can achieve that free-flowing movement you need when your head moves with your body. The reality is that your head is a heavy part of your upper body and must move with your upper body.

I believe the myth of the still head originated from the professionals who "felt" like the head stayed still when they swung, and they taught what they felt. This one-liner is an old wives tale. It has stuck for years, but that doesn't make it true or of any importance in learning a good swing. Let your head move freely with your body. Make no attempt to keep it still.

"Keep your left arm straight" - Golfers have been told, "You must keep your left arm straight." The idea is that the straight left arm will ensure contact with the ball. That simply is not the case. Most good players bend their left arm during the swing. One of the golf magazines did an article on how much PGA Tour Players bend their left arm during the back swing. It was quite an amazing collection of photos of some of the best Tour Players at the top of their swings. They all had some bend in their left arm.

Most golfers who hear this golf swing "law" interpret it as tightening the left arm until the blood stops flowing, in order to ensure that they hit the ball. All they succeed in doing is creating tension that will slow and distort the swing. The involuntary extension of the arm is a result of centrifugal force, a result of speed in the backswing. Don't try to straighten your left arm. Let the speed of your swing do it for you. Just relax and move the body.

"Keep your head down" - This is a term meant to describe the placement of your head at address and during the swing. It is an unspecific direction, so we are not exactly sure what position your head should be in during the swing. Should you tuck your chin into your chest? Many golfers think "keep your head down" is very important and they wrongly think it must be carried out to the utmost. Good players, however, have their head held high at address and during the entire swing. You need room for your body to move without any restriction from the position of the head.

Golfers with bifocal glasses tend to lower their heads too much in an effort to look through the top part of their glasses to see the ball. If you are doing this, get a pair of glasses that don't have the bifocal. Your head will be held higher and that will free up your shoulders and improve your swing.

"You must never, never look up" - Golfers have been told for ages to "watch the club hit the ball." Immediately after every poor shot you hit, all of your friends say, "You looked up." If your objective is just to hit the ball with the club, then by all means watch the ball until the club hits it and never bother to see where it goes. If, however, you have read the first part of this book and you realize that your objective is to deliver the ball to the target in order to score low, give up ever trying to watch the club strike the ball.

We get a lot of misinformation about this from still photos of Tour players as they strike the ball. Good players are in no way conscious of seeing the club strike the ball. It just appears that way, especially in still photos. Two of the very best golfers, David Duval and Annika Sorenstam, rotate their heads to the target well before the club gets to the ball.

This myth has been applied in other sports. I remember watching Wimbledon tennis on TV with my Dad. John McEnroe was doing the color commentary and Pete Sampras was playing. McEnroe commented on how Sampras "watched the ball right into the racket". Within 10 minutes of that comment, the newspaper came and the front page had a close-up picture of Sampras hitting a return shot. The ball, coming to him, was eight inches from his racket, but Sampras was already "looking up" at the spot where he wanted the ball to go. Like good tennis players, good golfers are more interested in getting the ball to the target than getting the club on the ball. Many would say, "They can do that because they are good." I say, "They are good because they do that." Good players must think about delivering the ball to the target, so think like a good player.

Looking at the spot on the ground where the ball has been has no redeeming value. You just lose a lot of balls, hit lots of short, crooked shots and score much higher than you should. You are free to look up as soon as you start the downswing, just like Duval and Sorenstam. They don't miss the ball, and you won't miss the ball. They are two of the best golfers ever. Their intention is to deliver the ball to the target. As you change your thinking to reflect an expanded and more correct objective -- delivering the ball to the target -- you will give your body and head permission to move freely to meet your objective. Once again, correct thinking yields a correct motion or swing.

"You must have a slow backswing" - This is a "law" that only refers to higher handicappers. The Tour Player's backswing is as fast as the downswing. I have never heard of a tennis player being told to make a slow windup (his backswing), and he has to hit a moving ball. Imagine a baseball pitcher making a slow windup so he can throw the ball exactly to the catcher's glove.

Did you ever see Ben Hogan or Nick Price swing? Their entire swings are very quick. I'm sure they didn't get that slow backswing lesson. Your whole swing must be a single speed and it must be quick enough to have your arms swung by the movement of your body. If your backswing is too slow, the muscles of your arms must make your arms move. That destroys relaxation. Again, if your backswing is slow, your body is prepared for a slow downswing. But you're not going to make a slow downswing if you want the ball to go a long way. Consequently, rather than a single-speed swing, you will start your downswing with a sudden great effort. Again, it's your arms trying to do all of the work, and you will hit a short, crooked shot.

"Turn in a barrel" - It's a little tricky to know exactly what's meant here. This is another inexact term. Does this mean turn the whole body like a corkscrew? No good Tour Player does that, and for good reason. The body is capable of moving athletically from side to side, but that's not possible if you are also trying to turn. In reality, there should be no attempt to turn your body.

As you try to turn, a reverse weight transfer takes place. Your weight goes to your left foot rather than your right foot and the toe of your right foot comes up in the air, taking away your power source. The strength of your body, your legs, is no longer of any value. You must not think of the body as a solid cylinder and try to turn it to gain strength. Your body will become stronger during the swing as you transfer the weight as was described in Chapter Ten. Your shoulders will rotate naturally, but never try to turn your entire body.

These are the myths we've heard so often that they seem to be facts. Now that you understand the foolishness of these "laws" I hope you will not be inclined to think they are something you must follow. Further, I hope you'll realize they are of no value. When my students hit a good shot I often say, "Nice shot; you looked up!"

PGA Tour story - best round.

Tom Weiskopf shot 64 the first round of the Greater Greensboro Open in 1974. *The next low score was 73.* The day was cold and windy. It was about 35 degrees and the wind blew hard enough to blow down the club house score board. It was held up with 4x4's. Tom held on to his nine shot lead and won the tournament. It was a tough day to break 90 let alone shoot 64. This has my vote for the best round of golf.

15

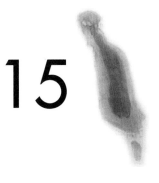

Let

You will see the word "let" used many times in this book. It was used with a definite purpose and definition. I want you to know exactly what I mean when I use this word and the connotations it implies. The dictionary defines the word as follows: To give opportunity to or fail to prevent and to free from or as if from confinement.

I intend the word as a freeing word, one that will get you out of your own way and keep you from interfering with the natural way your system functions. The word means for you to *allow* your system to work its magic. Most golfers are trying to *make* the body work perfectly and make shots happen rather than "*letting*" them happen. The harder you work and the more you try, the more you will inhibit the natural functioning of your body. Your job is to pick the right club and figure out the right shot, then get out of the way and let your system take over.

To let your system work its wonders requires trust. It's not really trusting your swing, like we hear so often, but trusting your *system* to create the swing that is needed for the shot in front of you. The shot you are faced with is brand new; you have never hit that exact shot before. As you get out of the way and trust your system to work the way it is capable of working, you will succeed. You will learn that your system is one of your best friends. So LET it work!

16

Think Low

Low scores? Yes. All golfers think about low scores. I'm going to encourage you to think about low shots as well.

As you gain an understanding of the five principles, there are two drills that will help you apply these ideas to your swing and game -- without you trying to micro-manage your body. The first drill is to learn to hit low shots.

I know, some of you are saying loudly to me that you do hit low shots -- too low. We are not talking about shots that roll along the ground. We're talking about lower than normal shots that get in the air. It's not so difficult to hit low, airborne shots. On windy days on the Tour, Linda, my wife, would see me off with this little bit of wisdom. "Hit it low,

24. All swings should be made with the intention of hitting low shots.

Your intension should be to hit every shot low

but get it off the ground." She understood the difference.

Shots that roll along the ground are the result of trying to get the ball up in the air. Swinging up at the ball to get the ball airborne will actually cause you to top the ball and hit the "worm burner." On the other hand, trying to hit a lower than normal shot will actually create a solid shot and cause the ball to get comfortably into the air.

Trying to hit low shots is a great learning drill. I discovered it one afternoon when I was working with a student who was having a tough time hitting a three wood off the ground. He kept hitting low-rollers because he wanted to lift the ball in the air. The way he saw the shot was to have the club come slightly up at the ball to lift the ball up into the air. Because he was trying to swing the club up at the ball, he was striking the ball with the bottom of the club and kept hitting the ball along the ground. I tried all the conventional techniques to get his body to do the right things, to absolutely no avail. Finally, I asked him to hit a shot no more than 100 yards and knee-high; try to hit it just above the ground. He hit the first one solid and in the air. His mouth dropped open in amazement. From that moment on he had no trouble with the three wood off the ground. A new and very effective learning drill was born.

What happened that improved his swing? He did all the things with his body that I wanted him to do to get the ball into the air. Since I had asked him to hit a specific type of shot, his focus was on the shot and not the swing. He didn't try to micro-manage his body during the swing; his body was not even in his thoughts as he swung. He was 100% focused on a very specific shot result: hitting the ball knee-high. His body moved in such a way to create the exact shot he wanted. Focusing on hitting a low shot causes four or five things to happen with the body during the swing that are very positive, without thinking about them or even knowing what they are. Golfers will ask what to do with their bodies to hit it low, but I won't tell them. Once they know what the body does to hit low shots, their focus is back on the body and the swing rather than the shot. *To know is to micro-manage* the body. **To know is disaster.**

From this we learn something very valuable. As you focus on the desired result, the type of shot you want, rather then the process which creates that result, you will be successful. That simply means that as you become totally focused on the shot and not the swing, your "system" will create in your body exactly what is necessary to generate the result you desire and envision. In this case, trying to hit low shots will make the body do many things you want it to do in order to generate a good swing which results in good, solid shots.

From now on, all swings should be made with the intention of hitting low shots, even if you are trying to hit a shot with a sand wedge straight up over a tree to a green. The swing should bemade as if you want the ball to go low along the ground. Adjust the face of the club so the ball will get up quickly.   If you will just do this and transfer your weight, your ball striking will improve instantly and permanently.

Did you ever realize where a great many of the best golfers and ball strikers learned to play golf? Many are from Texas, Florida, Oklahoma, California and England, some of the windiest places in the world. They were forced to learn to hit low shots. Could it have had any positive effect on their swing and their ball striking? Absolutely.   Byron Nelson and Ben Hogan are two great examples.

Here's an exercise which will help your swing function correctly, *without* your consciously thinking about your body and what it is doing: Get your seven iron and hit a few 50 yard shots, keeping the shot knee-high or lower. That's what you want for your plan and your "picture." The ball will go a little higher than your knees, but you keep it as low as possible and keep trying to hit it lower. You will hit solid shots and they will go further than 50 yards, but don't force the distance. This is a superb learning concept because it makes you focus only on the result and not on how to make your body move. As a result, it gets all the things done that you need to do with the body in order to hit solid, good shots. Think this way with all your clubs, all the time. That includes the driver, the wedges and the putter. The only clue I will give you is this: at impact the loft of the club must be reduced from its normal loft.

You have just learned to hit good solid shots and not

think about the body. I heard a story on the radio that helps illustrate this point. The interviewer was talking to a magician. He told all the stagehands that he knew they would eventually figure out how each trick was done. They could tell the secret to anyone --- except the magician. If they were to tell him they knew that the trick was done with the right hand going into his pocket, while the left hand was doing something else, he could no longer do the trick on an unconscious level. He would be aware of and think about his hand while he was doing the trick. When the move became a conscious move the audience would see it.

I avoid talking about the body positions during the swing in order to keep the golfer's thought off his body and on the shot so the swing can be made unconsciously. Being conscious of the target and the shot are OK. Trying to create a swing while thinking about the body will create a poor swing and a poorer shot.

Another good learning drill is to throw golf balls 20 to 25 yards. This is a second drill to help you apply the principles to your swing and game. It is simple but it has helped many of my students incorporate the principles into their swing without thinking about the body. Throw golf balls about 30 yards with a complete overhand throwing motion. This is a great way to get a sense of the athletic motion, which is the same motion as the golf swing. Throw some balls, make some practice swings, and then hit some shots. If your shots are not good, throw some more balls, make some more swings and then hit some more shots. Don't think about the specifics of what the body is doing during the motion, just throw or hit the balls to a spot.

I was teaching a 15-year-old who hadn't gotten his full growth yet. We played nine holes and I was impressed with his ability to play the game. His shots were accurate and he knew how to think. When we finished the nine holes, I complimented him on his play and asked him if he thought any part of his game needed help. He said, "I want to hit it longer." His assessment was correct and I knew he could do it.

We went to the range. I didn't want the young man to ever be conscious of what his body was doing during the swing. He was a baseball player. My "instruction" was simple. I asked him to throw 10 golf balls to a target about 30 yards away. When he finished, I asked him, "Is your golf swing the same motion you use to throw a ball?"

"No, not at all."

"Then make a golf swing that is the same as your throwing motion," I said.

He took some practice swings and copied the throwing motion exactly, even the picking up of his left foot during the backswing. The shots he hit with the new concept went 20 to 30 yards further than his old golf swing. The final result; a very happy young man.

This throwing drill has helped many of my students. Give it a try.

17

Incorporating the Principles Into Your Game

Now let's apply these five principles so you can perform them easily. We'll begin with the address position. You will need a club; your seven iron is the club of choice. Now we're going to get you into that good address position described in Chapter 8. To make sure your feet are shoulder-width apart at the inside of your heels, measure your shoulders with your club. Then, keeping that measurement, put your club between your heels and spread your feet that distance apart. With your feet set to the proper width, flex your knees and hold the club out in front of you with your elbows bent at your sides, and the club head slightly above the handle. Now, just bend forward and set the club on the ground. That's all there is to it. You're now in a powerful address position and you can make a real athletic swing.

Once you are in a good address position, you need to aim properly. You need to aim the club at a target and your body to the left of the target. Pick out a very distinguishable, but small target about 50 yards away. It can be a tree trunk or a flagstick. Now set the club behind the ball with the bottom line of the club perpendicular to the line from the target through the ball. If the line to the target is not clear, lay a club on the ground six inches outside the ball pointed at the target. When your clubface is aimed at the target, set your feet so the line through your toes points to the left of the target. The line through your toes can be as much left of the target line as you like, but not one inch to the right.

With this powerful address position and correct alignment you can begin learning the principle of weight transfer. To gain this understanding and a proper sense of the movement, I want you to do the same things as the students in a Concept Golf school. From a good address position with your seven iron in hand, lift your left foot off the ground a couple of inches. You are not trying to make a swing at this time. By picking your left foot up into the air, you have made 100% of your weight go to your right foot...without any turn. Now, put down your left foot and pick up your right foot. Once again, 100% of your weight will go to your left foot.

Pick up your left foot and then your right foot several times until you begin to sense a rhythm of the body and arms. You are still not trying to make a swing, but are simply moving the body by picking up your feet. You will see that the club is moving only because the body is moving and causing the club to move. It's not a swing at this point, but you can see that as the body movement is increased in distance and speed, a swing will be created.

Gradually allow enough speed and movement in the body to make the club swing to your waist on the backswing and again to your waist on the follow through. You are still picking your feet off the ground. Eventually you should be making full, effortless swings while you pick your feet up off the ground.

When you begin to feel like this amount of movement and lifting of your feet is not strange and that you are enjoying the sense of rhythm of the arms and body moving effortlessly together, start hitting some small shots with waist-high swings - still lifting your feet. You will be surprised because you will hit effortless shots that will be much longer than you would expect. After you have hit a few successful shots with the waist-high swing, enlarge the swing slightly and continue hitting shots. Remember, you are to continue lifting your feet.

Make no attempt to hit the ball any great distance during this stage of learning. Trying to force distance will cause your arms to take over, and that will destroy the coordination of your arms and body. This exercise is about learning to move your body effectively. You are learning to move your body as the good players do. You are also going to realize that you don't miss the ball because your body is moving. When you are comfortable with the smaller swing and are hitting good shots, increase the size of your swing to a full-size swing. I must caution you that it is not yet time to put your full effort into the swing. Plan on hitting your seven iron about 75 to 100 yards at the maximum. You're still picking your feet up in the air and learning to move the body.

A note of caution is appropriate here. It's easy to pick up your left foot during the back swing and just as easy during the downswing to pick up the right foot, unless the arms are doing some of the work -- then your right foot seems to be planted in the earth. Make sure your right foot is in the air at the end of the swing. If it is not, swing with less effort until you are finishing your swing with your right foot in the air.

After you are comfortable with this idea and you are making full but effortless swings and hitting some good shots, you can leave your toes on the ground when you swing. Don't swing flat-footed, but you no longer need to lift your feet completely off the ground. Some of you may want to continue picking up your feet, and that is quite all right.

With your body moving freely to the right and the left, it's time to make your arms function as a part of the body and keep them from fighting to try to take control of the swing. This is the fourth principle: relaxation. It's not possible for you to relax your shoulders until your body is moving to the right and the left as it should.

Relax your shoulders until your arms feel like they want to come out of their sockets. Bend forward and let your arms hang down completely relaxed and ready to fall to the ground. Now you are starting to relax those shoulders. You need to be aware that your system sometimes misinterprets relaxation of your shoulders. There may be times when you are trying to relax your shoulders, but instead, you relax your hands to the extent that you let go of the club during the swing -- but your shoulders are still tight. Another way your system misinterprets shoulder relaxation is through a slow backswing. A slow backswing may seem to be shoulder relaxation, but in reality it causes tension. As your arms move slowly the muscles in your shoulders must make your arms move. Just be aware that these two misinterpretations can occur and will prevent the shoulder relaxation you want and need to make great, consistent shots.

With your weight transfer causing your body to move so that your shoulders are relaxed, your arms will be swung into the backswing and dragged through the ball to the target. Let the club and arms go wherever they want to go; give up any sense of control. *It's a moment of complete trust that the club will somehow find the ball and move in the direction of the target.* The club does find the ball, and you will learn to trust it because it works so well. Your swing will start to feel light and effortless. Because you are swinging correctly, you will hit the ball very solidly and surprisingly far -- but don't try to force greater distance.

As you get comfortable with this swing based on the five Concept Golf swing principles, "let" your swing hit longer shots. Your target should be well within your normal distance, so just *let* your shots go over your target. A target at or beyond the end of your normal distance for that club will cause your arms to involuntarily work to make the ball go farther. You want to avoid any situation that will cause you to force your swing. You are making some *changes to your thinking* and you need to let the ideas take hold before you get too ambitious. Stay with your seven iron. Don't try to hit it over the target; you must just let the distance find you right now. Right now you are re-educating your system, so let it learn. I'll show you how to get more distance in *Golf Can't be this Simple - Playing the Game.*

With your body moving and your shoulders relaxed, now is the time to get your right leg and knee to work for you. It is tempting and quite easy to go to the outside of your right foot during the backswing. As you already know from an earlier chapter, your right leg is your real source of power, but it needs to be in the right position to help you. I have waited until after you are moving and relaxed to incorporate this principle because it can be restricting.

All you need to do is keep the right leg flexed the same amount as at your address position and keep your knee pointed at the ball during the entire backswing. This will keep your weight and pressure on the front inside part of your right foot (the ball and big toe) and keep your right foot in position so that your leg can reverse your swing at any moment. A word of caution is needed here. Because you want your right leg and knee to maintain their position, your body may want to quit moving to the right. It is imperative that you put all your weight on your right foot at the top of your backswing and keep your leg and knee flexed and pointed at the ball. You can do it; it's exactly the position you are in when you throw a ball. It's nothing new.

That's how you incorporate the principles into your swing. It's really a simple change of thought, as opposed to physical changes to your swing. It may take you a couple of hours to work through the five principles, but be patient with yourself because the rewards are going to be great. Please don't rush through the personal understanding of the five principles. You need to accept, trust, and develop a real understanding of these five principles. *They need to be a part of you and belong to you,* rather than simply being something you've read. You must express these fundamentals in your own way so that you can have your own swing, not a copy of someone else's swing.

These are the five principles -- the fundamentals that will anchor your swing on the solid rock of changeless ideas and make your swing work like a charm. Learn them and become good at them and they will serve you well.

18

A Lesson With John

In all the lessons I have taken as an amateur and a Tour Professional, only one teacher, Jimmy Ballard, explained the big picture of the swing before we went to the range. With a complete picture in mind there was a chance to incorporate the individual parts of the swing into the whole and make sense of the changes.

For some time now, I've understood that the only way to positively impact a better player's game is to play golf with the student, in order to identify the golfer's true problem areas so that they can be corrected. The assumption has been that to fix the swing is to fix the game. *Golfers' problems originate in their thoughts and must be corrected there.*

John is helping a student understand a concept

However, our first job is to accurately identify the trouble, and that will only reveal itself on the golf course. The problem may be in the swing, but why? The problem may be in the short game, but why? The problem may be in management, but why? Taking a look at the golfer's swing on the range will show me his swing in a very low-pressure situation, but will tell me nothing about him as a golfer and how I can help him improve his game.

In my eyes, you and all my students are par golfers. You are not a poor golfer trying to get better, except in your own eyes. If I, as your teacher, see you as an untalented golfer trying to become the model of consistency, I'm not going to be able to help you and you are not going to improve. My job really is to open your eyes to the reality of you being a par golfer at this moment.

Concept Golf teaches people to be better golfers so they can have fun playing the game. We begin with a half-hour conversation to learn about each other. I need to know a lot about you, both as a golfer and as a person. My questions are designed to learn how _you_ see your golf game, your swing, why are we here, your handicap, your goals, your golf strengths and weaknesses as you see them, your golf history, other lessons, family, other sports, employment, how committed you are, how much time you have for practice and golf and whether you can you use golf in business. At this point I determine our next step. If you are relatively new to golf or if there is a lot of confusion about the swing idea, we will probably go to the range. If you are a more accomplished golfer, we will play golf so I can learn about your golf game and see for myself the problems in your game that cost you strokes.

When we go to the range it's reasonable that you hit some wedges and seven irons so you can get the butterflies out of your stomach and I can see your "range" swing. Once I see your swing with a couple of different clubs and understand how you *think* of the golf swing, we can begin to give you the right ideas. Your swing will tell me what you are thinking about the swing, and the interview will tell me how the instruction needs to be structured so that it makes the most sense to you.

I will explain the five swing fundamentals of Concept Golf so you have a complete idea of the swing rather than just the disjointed parts and pieces. In order for you to have an effective swing, you need to have the correct, total understanding of the swing. That is the starting point. The total concept of the golf swing is presented in a logical manner so that the ideas are reasonable and make sense rather than nonsense. When it does make sense to you, you will be willing to accept the principles that will give you a swing that works. You will make great progress during the first lesson, hitting the ball further and more effortlessly than ever before.

Eventually we will play some golf. We will talk at the

end of our round and agree on a direction for your improvement. Often golfers do not know where or why they are losing strokes. As an outsider and teacher it's easier for me to identify and pinpoint the problem area or areas. A case in point is a friend of mine in Pennsylvania.

Rick Troutman called me one day and said he wanted to lower his average score from 73 to 69. He asked if I would come to his home and see what I could do. I've known Rick for several years and have played several rounds of casual golf with him. He's a good golfer and hits fairly long shots. When I arrived, we had a talk on the way to the course. The one thing he was quite blunt about was that I was not to work with his swing. I had no intention of working with his swing, just his game.

We played 18 holes the first day, then 36, 18, 18 and 18, spending no time on the range. He was hitting it to the right some of the time, and he did ask why. I gave him a one-sentence answer; that was the extent of my swing instruction. We worked on his pitching and talked about his putting, but the rest of the instruction was about *course management* and *Rick-management*.

He called two weeks later after winning a tournament and was very happy with the improvement and the instruction. He continued to play better and better. About two months later he called to tell me his average score was now 69. **Most golfers do not need swing instruction to have lower scores.**

Concept Golf has the goal of making you a better golfer with lower scores, not just improving your swing. As you become a better golfer, you probably will have a new, correct and understandable picture of the golf swing, but don't be limited to that. We will also need to look at your short game, course management and self-management.

Is this a true poem?

"I hate golf."
"I hate golf."
"I hate golf."

"Nice shot!"

"I love golf."

19

Your Objectives

Let's first agree on your objectives for your golf game. Most golfers I coach have certain goals in mind. As we talk, they share some of them. "I want to get the ball up in the air;" "I want a consistent swing that will hit the ball every time;" "I have a tournament tomorrow and I don't want to look like a fool," etc.

Most people think the objective in golf is to have a swing that consistently hits the ball, gets it into the air and keeps it out of the woods. This is a very limited view of golf and a big misconception. By that definition, a ball hit solidly, high in the air and 112 yards to the right of the fairway, but not in the woods, meets the objective. That won't work.

Your objective in golf should be to score low. A subset of the scoring objective is to have the object, the golf ball, go to the target. **Just wanting to hit the ball is a misstatement of your real desires and will keep you from becoming a good golfer.** So, let's agree that your goal is to score low. This includes having the ball go where you want it to go, rather than where it wants to go, most of the time. When the ball is not going where you want, your short game must pick up the slack and keep your golf score from looking like your zip code.

The golf swing is designed to move the object (the ball) to the target. Most golfers swing with fear -- fear of missing the ball -- so the whole design of their swing is to *not miss the ball* at all costs. That's a negative approach.

A good golfer has a swing that is truly designed to deliver the ball to the target because that's his objective. He assumes the hit and instead, concentrates on delivering the ball to the target with the proper kind of shot. From now on, rather than just trying to hit the ball, you are going to deliver the ball to a target -- just like the best players do. This is your *starting* point. Now you have a real goal; move the ball to the target in the distance. We will talk more about the target concept later, but it is a good idea to have agreement on what this game is all about. In football, basketball and some other games, score as high as possible. In golf, the objective is to score as low as possible.

With your objectives in mind, my first goal for your golf swing is to get you to the point where you have no sense of what the arms are doing at all, ever -- make your swing "armless." From there I am going to make you "bodiless" on the course. You should be playing the game with no thought about what the body is doing during the swing.

It's reasonable and necessary to have a good idea of where you want to end up in golf and how to know when you get there. Your goals and objectives need to be specific enough and definable enough to be able to know when to celebrate. That is not to say that your goals will not change as your game changes. No one comes to me saying they want to break 100 and when that is done they're satisfied forever. On the contrary, when they break 100 they are immediately on to the next goal of breaking 90. When Bobby Jones won the grand slam he quit competitive golf. That was the absolute pinnacle of golf and there was no other goal available for him as an amateur. It was time to retire from competition. When you get to your goals, we will talk about new ones.

By the way, when you get there, never say, "I've got it!" There are golf gods and they are not kind to those who say such things. Some oblique comment such as, "I'm beginning to understand," or "I'm getting better," is less likely to incur their wrath.

20

It's a Continuous Motion

The golf swing is a single-speed, continuous motion. Once you start in motion, you keep on moving until the finish, all at the same speed. It's the same concept as pitching a baseball, shooting a basketball, bowling a ball, hitting a tennis forehand shot or throwing a horseshoe.

The golf swing has taken on the aura of being something mystical and very scientific. It has been divided into parts and pieces in order to describe the motion with no regard to the whole idea. "Backswing" and "downswing" describe parts of the swing as if they are two distinct, separate parts, as if you are to make the backswing and when that is finished you start the downswing.

An athletic move like the swing is not, and cannot be, made up of separate movements, any more than the pitching motion or the basketball shot. **The backswing and the downswing overlap. It should not be distinguishable when the backswing ends and the downswing begins.**

Many golfers show up for lessons with a slow, controlled backswing because that is what they think is correct. Their friends have chided them every time they miss a shot for looking up and for making a quick backswing. When you have the opportunity, watch the Tour Players and you will see that most have a quick backswing. **A quick backswing is a necessity, not a problem.**

Problems occur when the backswing is slow. With a slow backswing, the *arms* must make the arms move as though they are independent of the body's motion. If the arms become independent, they control the movements of the arms and the body; you want exactly the opposite.

A good swing has the body in charge of the arms and results in a swift, effective motion that consistently delivers the ball to the target. A poor swing has the arms in charge of the body and that creates a slow, inaccurate swing that results in a short, crooked, ineffective shot.

A slow backswing has a real problem at the top of the swing where the change of direction occurs. The slow backward speed says to your whole system that the entire motion is going to be at that slow speed. We know that all golfers want great distance, and that's not possible if the downswing has the same slow speed as this super slow backswing. That slow back swing must erupt into a sudden desire for great speed and power. That's when we see that sudden violent jerk of the upper body that comes at the ball with all the strength of both arms. This makes the legs become "quiet followers" rather than "strong leaders." The club enters the ground an inch before the ball or the shot heads dead left or right.

So how do you create a quick backswing? **Make the backswing with your feet and legs moving quickly enough to cause your arms to be flung to the top of the backswing.**

The backswing actually begins with the forward press. That is a small movement of the body to the left which allows you to immediately recoil into the backswing. This allows you to start the swing from movement rather than from a dead stop. Your feet and legs will start the body moving, and that will cause the arms and club to swing to the top of the backswing.

As your arms approach the top of the backswing, your legs, which haven't been misled, will reverse the direction of the swing automatically. The legs will work out towards the ball and back towards the target to propel the body in that direction **with the arms following**. You will have the sense that the arms are being **dragged** through the ball to the target.

The legs know to do all the work if the backswing is quick enough. It's the same as throwing a ball: your legs work without you consciously knowing it or trying to make them work as long as your wind-up is sufficiently quick.

What should be the speed of your swing? It's obviously different for each golfer. It's determined by that personal metronome inside of you. Some metronomes barely move back and forth, others move at the speed of hummingbird wings. That internal metronome will determine your swing speed. Don't fight it.

Your instincts will tell you how fast to make your swing. All speeds are correct. Ben Hogan swung very quickly and he was good. Ernie Els swings very slowly and he is good, too. They both hit it quite long, so it not necessary to swing very quickly to hit long drives.

Your whole swing must be one speed, *your* speed. Don't try to make your swing speed the same as some Tour Player. Your swing must agree with your being, not some other player.

21

Taking it to the Course

A question on the lips of most golfers is how to take your good range game to the course. This is not as difficult as it may seem. You will usually ask this question after you have improved your ball striking on the range, to the point of some satisfaction. However, when you go to the golf course, you wonder where the good ball striker went. What happens and how can you avoid that?

Part of the problem results from the practice pattern of most golfers. Hitting a bunch of balls with a few clubs at a couple of targets (or with no target) is not practice. It is just exercise and swing tinkering. *Good practice is hitting no more than 2 shots per club per target per day.* **Practice making shots**, all kinds of shots you need on the course, to all kinds of targets in different conditions. This kind of practice will improve your ability as a golfer. The concept of practice will be covered in detail in the next Concept Golf book, *Golf Can't be this Simple...Playing the Game*

The other reason your good ball striking may leave you on the course is that the situation seems to be completely different from the range. You know what I mean...one ball, one swing, possible repercussions for an errant shot, trying too hard, fear etc., etc. So, how do you get the good stuff to the course?

Step one is good practice. Second, play more golf. Play more golf by yourself for a while. Playing alone has a couple of benefits: pressure-free golf with no one watching you, and the opportunity to hit a couple extra shots when needed. Go to the course in the middle of the afternoon, when it is quiet, and you will be able to play by yourself. Increase your confidence without the interference of other golfers and you'll soon be ready to play to your potential with others. *Practice golf rather than the swing, and you will take your good game to the course quickly.*

22

Teaching Children

I couldn't write this book without talking about another one of my passions -- teaching children to play golf. They are open, receptive and free of preconceived knowledge and useless information. They have never read a golf book or been told how hard the game can be. They think they can do it, and they can. They do.

All they want is a stick, some balls and a target to hit. Sometimes I will hit shots for them so they can watch me swing, and they get the general idea of how to hit the ball to a target. They learned to walk using the same method and succeeded. There was no instruction book or elaborate

The uncomplicated child

coaching for walking. They just watched and kept trying until they did it - their way. They even crawled before they walked, and fell down a few times after they learned to stand.

Children do the same in golf. They miss the ball for a while, but that doesn't faze them. They instinctively know their misses are educating the body more than the hits. They need some space and time to work through some of the tough spots.

Golf is rarely a game that yields immediate expertise, and it's no exception with the kids. They are going to miss the ball for a while, but that's OK. They will miss the target for a while, but that's OK. Let them work through some of this stuff on their own. It's good for them.

If your child has any interest in the game take him to a Tour event -- preferably a Senior event where the galleries are smaller. Walk nine holes (or even 18) with a good player. Ask your child which player they like and follow that player. Let your child watch a very good player play the game. If you stand at the practice tee for a while and just watch all the players hit balls, your child will get a pretty good sense of the golf swing. **Say nothing about how you think the swing works - they don't care and you may give them incorrect information.** Your child will learn by watching good players play -- just like he learned to walk -- not by elaborate words of instruction.

Kids teach adults. Watch their joy at a good shot. I watched a 6-year-old tee up a ball and keep swinging at it with his iron. He must have swung five or six times and finally he hit it. He bent over, picked the tee out of the ground and blew the sand off the end of the tee like a successful champion. There was no self-condemnation because he missed the ball a few times, only the joy of success. He wasn't counting, but he was impressed with the good shot. It was fun, and he thought he would try it again sometime. I like his attitude. After all, it's just a game. The best game ever devised.

Masters facts

Jack Nicklaus has won the Masters more than any other golfer. He won six times: 1963, '65, '66, 72, '75, and 1986.

Arnold Palmer is the second most frequent winner. He won four times: 1958, '60, '62, and 1964.

23

Summary

There you have it: Exactly what you need to understand in order to develop a good, consistent, effective and efficient swing. It's simple; it's easy and can be learned in a matter of hours. It will take a little longer to become very proficient at it, but you will be pleasantly surprised at how quickly you will be hitting good shots. At first glance the five principles may not seem like enough. There are only five fundamentals that create an effective golf swing, it may not sound complicated enough for something that seems as difficult as the golf swing.

We have bypassed all the hundreds of specific body positions deemed "necessary" by many people. However, these five principles generate every positive effect and every positive position you want in your swing, without trying to forcibly create them. This is easy, especially compared to trying to micro-manage the body into several hundred exact positions in the one-and-a-half-seconds of the swing. Understand the principles and start making some practice swings to implement these ideas that will revolutionize your golf game.

What is really great is that these principles are the same for the entire short game. Next, we'll apply these ideas to the short game. You will learn the short wedge, the chip, the sand shot and putting. A good long game is fun but a good short game is the scoring part of this game.

We have been given 14 clubs and just one swing. That certainly makes things easier, doesn't it? **Three of these clubs are more important to use well than all the others.**

They are the **pitching wedge**, the **putter** and your **driving club**. Notice that two of those clubs are used in the short game. Become very good with the wedge and very, very good with the putter, and you will score low. It's as simple as that. Typically, golfers will spend 90% of their practice time on the driver, 5% on the wedge and 1% on the putter. I know... we're missing 4% of the 100%; that practice time is spent watching the Golf Channel.

Here is something that might interest you about some of the short game material you will learn. After playing a practice round at the Sammy Davis Jr. Greater Hartford Open, my caddy, Joe, a friend who normally caddied for Al Geiberger, thought I could use some help with my chipping and short wedge shots. This was one of those unforgettable moments of special friendships on the Tour.

This time the friend was a caddie who shared what he had with me. Ray Floyd owed Joe some money, so he asked Ray to spend some time with me that afternoon to teach me to be better at chipping and pitching. Ray is the best with the chip shot and the pitch shot. He must have owed Joe some serious money because he spent three hours with me that afternoon. The chipping instruction you will get is the result of the education I got at the hands of Ray Floyd that afternoon in Hartford.

PART II

THE SHORT GAME

24

The Pitch Shot

The pitch shot is that little shot golfers use to make birdies possible and salvage pars. This shot gets a lot of use during a round of golf. The golfer who can hit these little wedge shots well will always keep his score low.

The pitch shot is less than a full swing, and is taken with the pitching wedge (or in some cases the sand wedge) and requires accurate judgment of distance. This is in contrast to full shots which require you to select the right club and then make a full swing. With a pitch shot, the club is a given and the distance is a variable. Once you've got the fundamentals, I'll tell you how to hit it the appropriate distance.

You'll be happy to know that the principles you learned for the full swing also apply to the short wedge shot. This is quite a revelation for most golfers, as they are under the impression that short shots require a very still body, as opposed to one that moves freely. All these myths will be debunked by the great results you'll be getting with your shots. The principles are the same for all clubs! You ask, "Even the putter?" The answer is "Yes!"

There will be some slight modifications in the address position. Your feet need to be closer together than with the full swing and the line through your toes needs to be more left of the target; about a 45-degree angle to the left of the target line. There should be slightly more weight on the left foot than on the right foot at address. Depending on the length of the shot, your hands will go down the grip; the shorter the shot the shorter the club. The ball is played slightly closer to your left foot, the same as all the other shots. Otherwise the address position is the same as with a full swing. The alignment of the feet is more to the left of the target but the bottom line of the club is still perpendicular to the target line.

Proper weight transfer is every bit as necessary in the short shots just as with the full shots. If you utilize proper weight transfer and let your body do the work, you can finesse a delicate shot. However, if your arms do the work in your short swing, you will have difficulty hitting the ball the

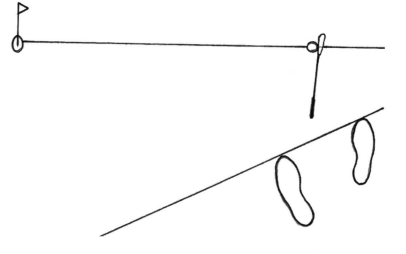

Stance for a good pitch shot

appropriate distance. Make a big body motion for little shots and you will be pleasantly surprised at your control of the distance. Both knees will move as your weight is transferred, just like the full swing. Relaxed shoulders are required for all shots in golf, and the little wedge shot is no exception.

Relaxation will let the arms and club find the perfect plane and the appropriate size of backswing for every shot. Tension in the arms and shoulders is what ruins most poor golf shots.

Relaxation causes the hands to be ahead of the clubhead at impact in every good golf shot

The following was stated in the chapter on relaxation, but it is important enough to restate it here as it applies to the wedge as well. **One of the very important by-products of the shoulder and arm relaxation is that the hands will -- and they must -- be ahead of the club head at impact and well into the finish. The club head never passes the hands in any good golf shot.**

The club head will solidly strike the ball when the hands are ahead of the club head at impact. This is something that can only be produced by relaxation. So relax and let's start hitting some very quality short wedge shots. Move your body and your arms follow. This sounds pretty simple --- and it is!

As you incorporate proper weight transfer in your swing, you will notice that your club will start hitting the ground after it strikes the ball. That is normal and good. We call that dislodged ground a divot. This should happen with full swings with irons as well as with short wedge shots, but not with the driver off the tee. This is a function of the body transferring the weight to the left foot, dragging the club and arms and causing the low point of the swing to be past the point where the club strikes the ball.

The right leg and knee must function the same way in the small swing as in the full swing. The leg should stay flexed and the knee should point at the ball during the backswing. The right leg is responsible for changing the body's direction back through the ball.

Because the principles of the Concept Golf swing are truly principles, they apply equally to all variations of the golf swing. The short shot is simply a variation of the full swing with exactly the same fundamentals.

A good drill that will establish the pitch-shot motion in your thinking is to toss a golf ball underhand to a small target 15 yards away. This is basically the same motion used in the short pitch shot. Tossing a few balls, along with your understanding of the five principles, will educate your system and have you hitting good pitch shots quickly.

Perfect golf story!

A perfect round of golf is one in which the golfer hits all fairways, all greens in regulation and has no three putt greens. Paul Harvey told the following story.

Two professionals and two amateurs had a friendly match at Spyglass Hill in CA. It was Ben Hogan and Byron Nelson against Ken Venturi and E. Harvey Ward. The professionals won by one shot on the 18th hole. All four had perfect rounds of golf and all four shot under 70.

I asked Harvey Ward to confirm this story and he simply said, "We all played pretty well that day."

25

Pitch the Right Distance

Now that you understand the idea of the less-than-full swing, the next challenge is having the ball go the right distance. The distance of these shots is limited and specific. If the flag is 22½ yards away, how do you hit a shot 17 yards that will roll up next to the hole? This is the question you face.

What must you do to hit the ball the distance you want it to go? Is it reasonable to consciously restrict the size of the back swing or make some other mechanical alteration? Do you take the club back to 10 o'clock if you want the ball to go 40 yards? This way of judging distance has been given lots of ink - but it certainly is not a fool-proof method and it requires more of that micro-management -- thinking of the body when you must be thinking about the shot and the target.

In order to help you understand how you can get the ball to go the correct distance, we will talk about throwing a horseshoe. If you've ever thrown horseshoes, the light goes on almost immediately. For those who have not thrown a horseshoe, I will give you three balls and ask you to throw them to me as I start walking away. I stay close for the first throw, further away for the next, and somewhat further for the last. Then I would ask, "With all distances being different, how did you know how far back to make your arm go to get the ball to me each time?" The reactive answer is that you just saw where I was and threw the ball to me, without knowing anything about what the arm was doing.

It's exactly the same with horseshoes. You make no conscious decision about the arm when making a throw for specific distance. The same ideas apply to the short wedge shot.

So, just how do you hit the ball the exact distance you want? We have a very sophisticated "system" and if we will allow it to work, it will work just like it does for us all day, every day. It's only when we try to "make" it work with the forebrain that we cause problems. It's the same "system" that gets you across the busy street. As you look down the road and see a car coming, your system subconsciously calculates the speed of the car, the distance it will travel and the distance you can cover in the time remaining. That's very sophisticated stuff and you have done it successfully every time. I can tell because you are reading this book and you are not under some car's tires.

To have the ball go a specific distance with a less-than-full-swing you simply need to feed the information into the system and let it work. That means you must spend a lot of time looking at the target, determining exactly where you want the ball to land, until the system figures out how much swing you need to make the ball go that distance.

It's reasonable to practice this shot from different distances and under different conditions to help the system learn. However, we must be careful to let the system work. We must never try to micro-manage the system or motion. Instead, keep your thoughts focused on the target while you are swinging. This is true with all shots in golf. Spend 20 seconds looking at the target and one second looking at the ball. Don't pick out a huge place for the ball to land, instead pick out a spot the size of a large cooking pot. The more specific you get, the better your opportunity to hit the target. We'll talk more about the target concept later, but suffice it to say that, if you want to hit a house, pick out a single windowpane.

If you know exactly where the target is while you are swinging and exactly the kind of shot you want to hit, your system will manage your body and create the needed swing to deliver the ball the right distance. This is true for all shots in golf but it's more fun with the less-than-full swings around the green and the putter.

26

The Chip Shot

You will have a lot of fun learning this shot because you will get very good at it very quickly. This is the shot from the short grass from just off the edge of the green. The distance from the green can vary from a couple inches to a few yards.

The reason we chip rather than putt is because we expect to have the ball go in the hole. Putting through the long grass will throw the ball off-line and make judging the speed difficult. The idea is to hit the ball in the air just to the edge of the green and get the ball on the ground all the way to the hole, just like a putt. It should become a putt as soon as it hits the ground, never bouncing. Your seven iron should be the club of choice.

For your learning session, put your ball five feet from the edge of the green and choose a hole about 20 feet from the edge of the green.

In the address position the feet are very close together, heels almost touching, and the line through the toes is 45 degrees to the left of the target. The club head is aligned with the target line. The ball is played off the middle of the right toe, so it is way back in the stance. This is done to help take the loft off the club and to produce the low running shot you want. With the ball so far back in the stance, off the right toe, your hands will naturally fall forward of the club head. Since this is a very short shot, your hands should be at the bottom of the grip almost on the shaft. To preset t he conditions so the result is a low shot, put a little more weight forward on the left foot than on the right foot. Now that we've covered the address position, let's move on to the swing.

Even for such a small shot like the chip the stroke is made with the "big muscles." Once again, proper weight transfer is the major cause of the swing. With this small swing the weight transfer is not as obvious as the driver swing. It is seen in the movement of the knees.

If the arms try to move the arms, or the hands try to move the club head, they will destroy this shot just like they ruin a full swing. Relaxation will result in an impact position with your hands well ahead of the club head. This will de-loft the club and produce the very low-trajectory shot you need. It is absolutely necessary for your shoulders to be completely relaxed during this swing, just as with the full swing. With a little bit of practice, you will become very good at this and start expecting to make some of these shots during your rounds of golf. Have fun with this shot.

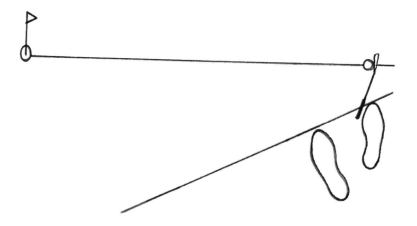

Stance for a perfect chip shot

In Concept Golf schools, we begin the chip shot session with a pitching wedge. We ask the golfers to hit chip shots from five-feet off the green to a pin that is 10 feet from the edge of the green. This is a low running shot just like the seven iron, and it is fun and a valuable shot to have in your bag. Depending on how far your ball is from the edge of the green and how far the pin is from the edge of the green, you can chip with any club from the four iron to the pitching wedge.

27

The Art of Putting

Putting is often depicted as a science, but it is an art. We are taking a Concept Golf view of the game, so you will get a look at putting from that perspective, rather than a so-called scientific approach.

To illustrate just how important putting is to your score, I ask this question: if you hit every green in regulation and two putt every green, what percentage of your shots would be putts? You're right, 50%. We'll begin by discussing the ideas behind the putting stroke, then move on to making practice fun.

Putting is simple: hit the ball into the hole. It's amazing how often golfers overlook that objective and get all tied up in the mechanics of the stroke. Just as with the full swing, the idea that improvement is found by changing the stroke is very seductive. Golfers at all levels fall prey to this kind of thinking. We will talk about the putting stroke in terms that will allow you to learn the ideas, not specific body positions, and get on with making putts.

Having the ball go the right distance is most important

There are two aspects to putting: line and distance. Most golfers take a lot of time and effort to get the line right and then leave the ball two-feet short or 10 feet past the hole. The reality is that the distance, or speed, is 95% of putting. With the exception of perfectly straight putts, even the line is mostly determined by the speed of the putt.

You won't be successful at putting if you read a putt to break right and it breaks left. However, if you do get a reasonably correct read, the amount of the break is determined by the speed of the putt. All putts can be straight if you hit them hard enough. Our focus is on three areas: 1) the correct ideas of the putting stroke, 2) determining the proper effort for the distance required, and 3) an understanding of what you are really trying to accomplish. As always, we will keep it simple.

Let's talk mechanics of the stroke for a moment. The putting stroke, body position and ball position are all very personal. Hold the putter any way you want. No rules. Stand any way you want. No rules. Put the ball any place in the stance. No rules. An observation: many of the very best putters have used an open stance. They can see the hole better. You must be relaxed, especially in the shoulders. Grip the putter gently.

The stroke is made with the biggest muscles possible. The putting stroke is the same basic motion as the driver swing. While you don't need the weight transfer from the right to the left for a putt on fast greens these days, you still should use the biggest muscles possible. Use the muscles in the lower back to cause the shoulders to be moved, so that the shoulders and arms can be completely relaxed. Do not use your arms to make the club move. Any time the arms make the arms move, you are asking for a poor shot.

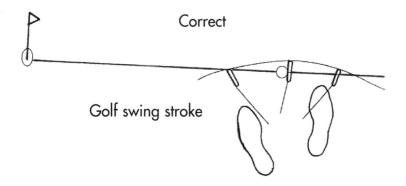

Correct

Golf swing stroke

Illustration 1

Today's traditional golf instructor tells you that you must be perfectly still and never look up during the putting stroke. These thoughts make your body freeze and cause the arms to do the work, creating a poor stroke. It is not necessary that you stay perfectly still while you putt. Some movement is fine and will not cause you to miss the putt or the ball. Bobby Locke moved his head when he putted and he beat the best in America primarily because he was a superb putter. Use the big muscles in the lower back to cause the shoulders to move and the arms will follow with sensitivity and reliability.

Because you use the muscles of the back to move the upper body, your arms and putter follow the same swing path as the driver. The backswing is slightly to the inside of the target line and the putter face seems to be open to the target line. As the club swings back past the ball, it will go slightly to the inside of the target line and the face will seem to close to the target line. The face is really square to the target line, but it seems to open and close slightly.

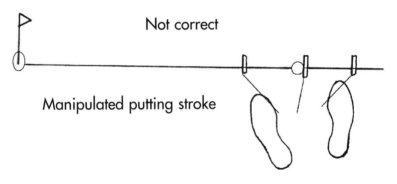

Not correct

Manipulated putting stroke

Illustratrion 2

There is a "scientific" approach these days which says the putter should always travel along a straight line back and through as if on a railroad track. This can only be done with contrived control of the direction of the club, with the arms taking charge and moving independently of the body. Again this focuses your thoughts on micro-managing parts of the body in order to have a prescribed swing direction that is incorrectly assumed to be the same for all golfers. The good putting stroke is a very small version of the full swing. It has all the same principles and must be done in your way.

Gravity causes the ball to follow the terrain of the green and go toward the lowest place on the green. Understanding the amount of slope and how the ball is affected by the slope at a given speed is called "reading" the green. With experience you will do this better and better, but the speed is what affects the line more than gravity. Let's talk about the speed.

How hard do you have to hit the ball in order for it to go the distance you want it to go? Once again, we return to your "system." Let's illustrate how your system works.

You have three golf balls and are going to quickly throw one to each of three people at different distances. How do you get the ball to go the right distance each time? You don't think about it -- you just look at each person as you throw the balls and they will go the right distance. You didn't throw any balls 20 feet past a person or 20 feet short. Your system works the same way in putting. As long as you know where your target is, you will hit the ball the needed distance. Most often you hit poor putts when you are focused on hitting the ball, or trying to make sure you perform the stroke in the latest prescribed manner, and forget about your target. It's really as simple as knowing where the hole is and hitting the ball into the hole.

Often I ask new students to look at the hole while they putt. If they have been playing golf for a while I get some very strange looks. By looking at the hole the player is totally focused on the target and their "system" goes to work, usually hitting the ball the correct distance and along the right line. After a few putts it becomes comfortable to look at the hole, and the results are better than when they were looking at the ball.

Eventually they want to look more conventional, so I ask them to take a practice swing looking at the hole. They look at the hole long enough to memorize where it is, glance at the ball and putt. As you hold the cup in your mind's eye while you putt, you will get the same effect as if you were still actually looking at the hole. For your "system" to work, it must know exactly where the target is all the time. Putt with the hole in mind and the ball will go the right distance.

All of you spend 50% of your practice time on the putting green, right? Probably not. Practicing putting is not usually fun! It is important, but standing on the putting green and hitting putts for hours is not very exciting. Let's change all that and make practice fun and worthwhile!

Let's talk about ways to practice putting that will be meaningful and fun. If it's not fun you won't do it, and if it doesn't help, you won't continue to practice. To consistently score low, you must become a very good putter from six feet and closer. I want you to focus on putts of this length and let the longer putts take care of themselves.

The first "game" requires just one person and four golf balls. Place them around the hole at one foot, opposite each other. Make those putts and reset the balls at two feet, then three feet, etc., all the way to six feet. If you miss a putt at any point you must start over at one foot. When you make them all from six feet, you can have lunch. This is also a very good diet until your putting improves.

There is a slight variation to this game which includes placing six balls, starting at one foot, in a slightly curved line one foot apart. Curve the line so there is room for your putter to swing. Keep putting until you miss and then start over. When you've made it from six feet, pick a different line to the same hole. When you make all the 6 footers from four angles, you can have lunch, or perhaps it's dinner.

The next game is more advanced. You may want to wait to play this game until you feel good about your putting. It needs at least two golfers, and five is too many. You'll like this game. I have played this many, many times and it is always a lot of fun and good for your putting to boot. It's called "21" and here is how it's played:

1. Each player plays with two golf balls and putts both balls before the next player plays.

2. All players play from exactly the same spot; a point can be designated by a coin or a tee.

3. The "honors" on the first hole are selected by chance; flip a coin or spin a tee. Thereafter, the player making the points on the preceding hole is the first to play and the others play according to whoever made the previous points. It's just like honors on the golf course. The order of play can be very important since stymies are the rule. The leading player chooses the next hole.

4. Stymies (not being able to move a ball to clear a line for the next player) are the rule; balls are left where they stop until all players have finished. Stymies also mean that if Player B hits Player A's ball and knocks it into the hole, Player A will get the points. If Player B also goes into the hole, he will get all the points and A will get no points. B can also knock A closer or further from the hole to add a point or take away a point.

5. Points are scored for the ball(s) of one player closest to the hole. If Player A has one ball closer than Player B's closest ball, player A earns one point. If player A has both balls closer to the hole than either of Player B's, Player A earns two points. Player B earns no points in either case.

6. Holes-in-one are more interesting. A hole-in-one is worth three points. However, if Player A makes a hole-in-one and Player B makes one on top of Player A, Player B gets six points and Player A gets no points. Only one person

makes points for a hole-in-one, regardless of the number of players. It is possible to make four points on a hole; a hole-in-one and a ball closer than any other player.

7. It is possible to earn one, two, three, four or six points on a hole with two people playing the game. Points can go higher with more people because of the hole-in-one rules.

8. The first player to 21 points or greater is the winner.

9. Any ball that leaves the green costs the player a point.

Option for later on: Any ball that is not within a putter length must be putted in the hole. If the putt is missed, the player loses a point.

With these games you can have fun and watch your putting improve. It will also give you the chance to putt under a little pressure.

Thoughts to ponder

Nonchalant putts count the same as chalant putts.

It's not a gimmie putt if you're still away.

It's surprisingly easy to sink a 50 foot putt when you lie 10.

28

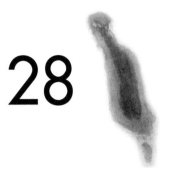

Sand Shots

Sand shots are not the most important shots in your bag because they happen infrequently. Further, as you improve your skills with the Concept Golf principles, sand shots will automatically improve as well. We'll cover two shots: the explosion from the green-side bunker and the long shot from a fairway bunker.

As an aside, the term "sand trap" is not a real term in golf. The rulebook deems it a hazard, specifically a bunker. The phrase "sand trap" is also quite negative in that the word "trap" gives one the sense that he is "trapped" and escape is difficult, if not impossible.

The explosion shot from a green-side bunker is an easy shot. It uses the same principles as the short wedge shot, with a few small changes. Your number one objective is to get your ball out of the bunker in one swing. You can get fancy later on, but for now you want to get out of the bunker on a reliable basis, with one swing.

Here's the address position for the explosion shot: stand as if the shot was a full swing, but with the line through your toes being 45 degrees left of the target. You do this to compensate for the more open clubface you will create. Your feet should be wide apart. Hold the club at the end. The ball is positioned just forward of center. Place slightly more weight on your left foot. Open the club face by spinning the club in your hands. Note: do not change the face angle by holding the club and twisting your hands. To provide stability during the swing, work your feet into the sand so that the insides of your feet are deeper.

The swing technique is the same as with all other clubs. Weight transfer is the foundation, so go to the right foot and then to the left foot. Keep the right leg flexed and the knee pointed at the ball. Make sure your shoulders are relaxed during the swing. The swing is a full-size swing that is more gentle than a driver swing. Your mindset should be to make a swing that would hit the ball about 50 yards from the grass. Hitting the sand, and not the ball, will deaden the shot more than you expect.

The sand wedge is constructed so that the trailing edge is higher than the leading edge to prevent it from digging deep into the sand. With the clubface open, you want the club to enter the sand about two inches behind the ball. Many students are timid about this shot, thinking the ball will go too far. To remedy this fear, go to a fairway bunker and explode a shot with a full swing. Even with a full swing, it won't go very far when you hit two inches of sand first.

How about the fairway bunker shot? The address position is basically the same as from the grass, except that you work your feet into the sand, with the insides of your feet deeper for stability. Place the ball more towards the right foot than the left foot by a couple inches. The objective here is to hit the ball and then some sand, but never sand and then the ball. This is in contrast to the green-side bunker, where you hit sand first. The swing is the same as if you were on grass. Weight transfer is still the dominant idea. Swing at about 80% effort to avoid your feet slipping. Take one club more than you would for this shot from the grass. You are going to aim the bottom line of the club at the middle of the ball and try to cut the ball in half. The idea is to not hit any sand before you hit the ball.

Rules note: The rules say you cannot touch the sand with the club before making the swing. You need to hold the club above the sand while preparing to hit a sand shot.

29

Your Swing Tools are Complete - Now Let's Play the Game!

Now that you understand Concept Golf's five swing principles, it's time to put them to use on the course. You have added a consistent swing and a solid short game to your arsenal. You can deliver the ball to your target with reasonable certainty.

Because you have a clear understanding of the swing and the short game, a few bad shots will not tempt you to look for new quick-fixes based on the latest tip or fad. You have a solid foundation which enables your swing and shot making to continually improve. You have a consistent swing

Learn how to play the game - *not* how to make
great golf swings

because you are not flitting from quick-fix to quick-fix. You know and understand the swing, and, that eases your mind. Rather than tinker with your swing, you now practice making shots.

Now you are ready to learn how to play golf. You need to learn what kind of shot is needed at what times, and under what conditions. You need to be able to hit a variety of shots with confidence and certainty. Many of these shots will be completely new to you.

While discussing the swing, we were concerned with the process -- the swing. As you learn about playing the game, you will seldom think about the swing or your body. Instead, you will learn to think about your target, the elements and the kind of shot you need to hit to deliver the ball to your target.

You should read the second Concept Golf book, _Golf Can't be this Simple -- Playing the Game_ as soon as possible. The second book will teach you how to play, plan and think like a PGA Tour Player. It will open your eyes, not only to course management, but also to your concept of yourself as a golfer. You will learn how to deal with the weather and what to expect from different lies and positions on the course. The objective of that book is to show you how to consistently score low, through planning and knowing how to handle a variety of situations.

This intent of *Golf Can't be this Simple - The Swing*, is to simplify the golf swing and make it easy for you to do. I want you to have more fun playing golf.

I ask you again to let me hear from you about your progress. Tell how golf is more fun for you. Let me know about your good scores and how the ideas of Concept Golf have simplified the swing. I also want you to feel free to ask questions about the ideas presented in this book.

Please contact me by email at: john@conceptgolf.com, visit the web page at www.conceptgolf.com, by snail mail at PO Box 152, Rolesville, NC 27571; or call me at (919) 570-9772.

Thank you for inviting Concept Golf into your golf game. You've got the swing -- now learn to play the game! Play well, play often, and have fun!

Additional Resources

The following schools are available with Concept Golf

<u>Players Schools:</u> Schools for golfers with a 10 or lower handicap. Learn how to play the game.

<u>Business Golfers School:</u> Learn the swing, the rules, the etiquette, and how to effectively use golf to grow your business.

<u>Swing Schools:</u> The golfer will learn how to make a swing that hits consistently good shots.

Experienced golf professionals are available to make your company outing very special. We also deliver speeches in the areas of the golf swing, the PGA Tour and using golf to grow your business.

Visit our website at <u>www.conceptgolf.com</u> for information about the Concept Golf videos and additional books and services.

 <u>Pioneer Communications Strategies, Inc.</u>, a public relations agency in Raleigh, North Carolina, headed by Frank Williams. Frank's specialties helped develop this book and the long term strategic direction for Concept Golf. Visit their web site at <u>www.pioneerstrategies.com</u>.

Order Form

Books:

Golf Can't be this Simple - The Swing $24.95

The five Concept Golf swing principles will make you a consistent golfer

Golf Can't be this Simple - Playing the Game $24.95

Learn how to play the game of golf well. Golf can be fun!

Videos:

The Full Swing - The Big Idea $29.95

A presentation and demonstration of Concept Golf's five swing principles

The Short Game $29.95

The five swing principles are applied through demonstration to putting, pitching, chipping and sand shots.

Company name_____

Name_____

Address_____

City_____State_____ Zip_____

Email_____

Please indicate the number of copies. Swing Book____Playing Book____

Full Swing Video_____Short game Video_____

Sales tax: Please add 6.5% for NC shipping addresses

Shipping: Book and Video Rate $4.00

Payment:

(   ) Check

(   ) Credit Card: Visa   Mastercard   (Circle One)

Card number_____

Name on Card_____Exp. Date___/_____

Telephone Orders: (919) 570 9772.

On-line Orders: www.conceptgolf.com

Postal Orders: Concept Golf, PO Box 152, Rolesville, NC 27571

Thank You

Order Form

Books:

Golf Can't be this Simple - The Swing $24.95

The five Concept Golf swing principles will make you a consistent golfer

Golf Can't be this Simple - Playing the Game $24.95

Learn how to play the game of golf well. Golf can be fun!

Videos:

The Full Swing - The Big Idea $29.95

A presentation and demonstration of Concept Golf's five swing principles

The Short Game $29.95

The five swing principles are applied through demonstration to putting, pitching, chipping and sand shots.

Company name_____

Name_____

Address_____

City_____State_____ Zip_____

Email_____

Please indicate the number of copies. Swing Book____Playing Book____

Full Swing Video_____Short game Video_____

Sales tax: Please add 6.5% for NC shipping addresses

Shipping: Book and Video Rate $4.00

Payment:

(   ) Check

(   ) Credit Card: Visa   Mastercard   (Circle One)

Card number_____

Name on Card_____Exp. Date___/_____

Telephone Orders: (919) 570 9772.

On-line Orders: www.conceptgolf.com

Postal Orders: Concept Golf, PO Box 152, Rolesville, NC 27571

Thank You

Gift Order Form

Books:

Golf Can't be this Simple - The Swing $24.95
The five Concept Golf swing principles will make you a consistent golfer
Golf Can't be this Simple - Playing the Game $24.95
Learn how to play the game of golf well. Golf can be fun!

Videos:

The Full Swing - The Big Idea $29.95
A presentation and demonstration of Concept Golf's five swing principles

The Short Game $29.95
The five swing principles are applied through demonstration to putting, pitching, chipping and sand shots.

Company name_____

Name_____

Address_____

City_____State_____ Zip_____

Email_____

Please indicate the number of copies. Swing Book____Playing Book____

Full Swing Video_____Short game Video_____

Sales tax: Please add 6.5% for NC shipping addresses

Shipping: Book and Video Rate $4.00

Payment:

(   ) Check

(   ) Credit Card: Visa   Mastercard   (Circle One)

Card number_____

Name on Card_____Exp. Date____/_____

Personalize to_____

Telephone Orders: (919) 570 9772.

On-line Orders: www.conceptgolf.com

Postal Orders: Concept Golf, PO Box 152, Rolesville, NC 27571

Thank You